THE
HANDCRAFTED
BURGER

THE HANDCRAFTED BURGER

MASTER THE ART OF CRAFTING
THE ULTIMATE GOURMET BURGERS

This edition published by Parragon Books Ltd in 2018
and distributed by

Parragon Inc.
440 Park Avenue South, 13th Floor
New York, NY 10016
www.parragon.com/lovefood

LOVE FOOD is an imprint of Parragon Books Ltd

ISBN 978-1-4748-9724-2

Printed in China

Edited by Hannah Kelly

Production by Fiona Rhys-Griffith

Introduction by Dominic Utton

New recipes, home economy, and food styling
by Lincoln Jefferson

Cover photography by Mike Cooper

New recipe photography by Mike Cooper
and Al Richardson

Additional images on pages 8–12 courtesy of iStock

NOTES FOR THE READER

This book uses standard kitchen measuring spoons and
cups. All spoon and cup measurements are level unless
otherwise indicated. Unless otherwise stated, milk
is assumed to be whole, eggs are large, individual
vegetables and fruits are medium, and pepper is
freshly ground black pepper, and salt is table salt. A
pinch of salt is calculated as $1/16$ of a teaspoon. Unless
otherwise stated, all root vegetables should be peeled
prior to using.

The times given are only an approximate guide.
Preparation times differ according to the techniques
used by different people and the cooking times may
also vary from those given.

Please note that any ingredients stated as being
optional are not included in the nutritional values
provided. The nutritional values given are approximate
and provided only as a guideline; they do not account
for individual cooks, measuring skills, and portion
sizes. The nutritional values provided are per serving
or per item.

For best results, use a food thermometer when cooking
meat. Check the latest government guidelines for
current advice.

Vegetarians and vegans should be aware that some
of the store-bought prepared ingredients used in the
recipes in this book might contain animal products.
Always check the packaging before use.

It is recommended that you do not consume more than
15 g of chia seeds per day.

CONTENTS

THE BURGER REVIVAL

Are burgers the perfect food? There's a pretty good argument that says so. They are quick, inexpensive, and easy to cook, as well as able to be adapted, added to, and experimented upon to suit just about any taste—and, of course, and most important, they're totally delicious.

There's a lot more to the humble patty and bun than many might think. The recent resurgence in the popularity of the burger is testament to that—from a wealth of dedicated restaurants serving weird and wonderful varieties to its presence on even the most upscale menus, burger-lovers have never had it so good.

But you don't need to eat out to enjoy the pleasures of a gourmet burger—and you don't even need to be especially good at cooking to create them. That's where this book comes in. Over the next pages, you'll find 100 simple recipes for creating your own delicious burgers, sides, and sauces at home, as well as an astonishing number of flavor combinations to be sure your creations are just spectacular as anything made in a professional kitchen.

From straight up Traditional Hamburgers and Pork Belly Sliders to Bacon-Wrapped Chicken Burgers and Turkey Gorgonzola Burgers, creativity is given free rein—and with flavorings that include everything from peanut butter and teriyaki sauce to avocado and jackfruit (the latter is available in Asian grocery stores), there really is no limit to what can be done.

Burgers are by no means limited to meat-eaters—and inside this book you'll find mouthwatering variations on the form, using ingredients as diverse as quinoa, sweet potato, halloumi, and beet. Who wouldn't be tempted—vegetarian, vegan, or otherwise—by a Kale & Black Bean Sloppy Joe burger, served in a homemade bun with garlic fries and guacamole?

Sides are not forgotten—and move well beyond fries. With easy recipes for salads, coleslaws, onion rings, plus a range of fries that go above and beyond the usual (Smoky Paprika Sweet Potato Fries, anyone?), the whole meal is catered for. There are even simple steps for creating your own ketchups, mustards, salsas, hummus, and mayonnaise.

And the best thing? Delicious they may be, but these burgers are not the "guilty pleasure" you might assume them to be. Each recipe includes a nutritional analysis, so you can see exactly what you're eating. Believe it or not, many are a lot healthier than you would think.

Making burgers is not only easy—it's fun. Whether you're selecting the right cuts of meat, learning to fashion the perfect patty, experimenting with different cooking methods, getting creative with your sauces, toppings, and other ingredients, or whipping up a selection of perfect sides, there's everything you need here to be sure no barbecue, dinner party, or family get-together will ever be the same again.

So roll up your sleeves, strap on the apron, turn up the heat, and get your taste buds in gear—the following recipes will change the way you look at the humble burger forever.

GETTING STARTED

True to its humble origins, the hamburger is a low-tech food requiring not much more than a sharp knife for slicing tomatoes and a skillet, broiler, or barbecue. Here is the only equipment you'll really need:

- Mixing bowls
- Spatula for flipping burgers
- Knives for slicing tomatoes (serrated work well), lettuce, and other accompaniments
- Whisk for making sauces, such as mayonnaise

- Skillet or ridged grill pan. Look for heavy pans, which have better heat transfer, to create a better sear on your burgers
- Broiler pan and rack
- Gas, electric, or charcoal barbecue
- Meat grinder or food processor (optional) to make the freshly ground beef

HOW TO MAKE THE PERFECT BURGER PATTY

Burgers are incredibly easy to prepare, and the only really important step, beyond not overcooking them, is forming the patty. The main thing to avoid is overworking the meat, which can result in tough burgers instead of tender and juicy ones.

Fresh ground chuck beef is the easiest to work with, because it's both dry enough and sticky enough to bind well. Ground turkey, chicken, and pork can be much wetter than beef and, therefore, harder to shape, but adding some bread crumbs can help alleviate that problem. Also, wetting your hands while forming the patties helps. The same applies to vegetarian burgers, which can be wet and difficult to shape.

To form patties, place the meat in a bowl, add all of the seasonings at once, then mix—preferably with your hands—just long enough until the seasonings are completely integrated.

Divide the meat mixture into even portions, then gently form each portion into a patty. If possible, make the patties slightly wider than the buns, because they will shrink during cooking. For the same reason, it also helps to make the edges of the patty thicker than the center, or to add a dimple to the center of the patty, so that when the meat contracts, the patty will end up an even thickness when it's cooked.

HOW TO COOK
THE PERFECT BURGER

Quick cooking methods with high, dry heat are the best way to get burgers beautifully browned on the outside and juicy inside. Each recipe in this book specifies how to cook the burgers for best results, but you can adapt the recipes to use any of the methods listed below.

FRIED AND GRILLED

This is the traditional diner method of cooking burgers, which involves a hot skillet or ridged grill pan and some cooking fat. The burgers cook over medium–high heat until they develop a golden-brown crust.

STEAMED

Steaming takes frying one step farther to keep the meat extra-moist. While frying, just cover the burgers with a lid to finish cooking.

BARBECUED

Charcoal barbecues provide a smoky flavor, but gas ones are easier to use. To check the heat level of your grill after preheating, hold your hand about 1 inch above the cooking grate. The time it takes to get uncomfortably hot determines how hot the grill is:

HIGH: About 3 seconds
MEDIUM–HIGH: About 5 seconds
MEDIUM: About 7 seconds

SMOKED

An aluminum foil pouch of wood chips creates smoke that infuses its flavor into burgers cooking in a covered barbecue. Different kinds of wood create a variety of flavors, so experiment. Smoking on a barbecue requires a barbecue with a lid or hood.

BROILED

Broiling is an easy, low-mess method that works especially well for fish, poultry, or vegetarian burgers, which tend to stick to the grate. It is also a great alternative for any recipe that calls for grilling when the weather doesn't look good for outdoor cooking.

HINTS & TIPS

Choose meat with the right amount of fat. Because burgers cook over a relatively high heat, using lean meat can result in dry, tasteless burgers. The preferred fat amount for beef is 18–22 percent, and ground turkey or chicken from leg meat is the best choice for poultry burgers when it comes to flavor and texture.

You can grind almost any kind of fresh meat yourself. Beyond beef, you can use the same method with chicken, lamb, pork, or turkey. Just cut the meat into 1-inch cubes and chill first to avoid ending up with pureed meat (particularly important with poultry).

If you prefer your burgers well-done, add grated cheese or finely chopped vegetables to the meat to keep it moist. Some people even add chipped ice to their meat, around two crushed ice cubes per 1 pound of meat (these need to be cooked immediately; otherwise the ice cubes will melt).

Always preheat before cooking. Whether using a skillet, broiler, or barbecue, make sure the cooking surface is hot before you add the patties. This prevents it from sticking and results in the best browning.

Be gentle with the meat. If your burgers come out a bit tough, it means that you probably handled the meat too much when forming the patties.

Choose your buns wisely. Most burger aficionados prefer softer buns or bread that doesn't fight with the meat or vegetable patty. If you want to warm the buns, don't let them get too dry and toasty. You can try making your own buns following the recipes on pages 200 and 202.

Don't mess with the patties. Some cooks like to flip their patties several times and can't help but press down on them with a spatula. This only toughens them up.

A few recipes call for an item on the barbecue to be covered. In these instances, it is best to use a barbecue that has a fitted lid or hood. Ultimately, this feature enables an intense smoky flavor to penetrate the food and also provides more even cooking.

If your patty isn't binding—this can be a problem, especially with poultry, fish, or vegetarian burgers—try adding bread crumbs to the mixture. Chill the formed patties for 15 minutes to help them stay together.

The cooking times given for each recipe are only for guidance. Cook your burgers to your preference, but make sure pork and chicken are cooked properly. Cut into the middle to check that the meat is no longer pink. Any juices that run out should be clear and piping-hot, with visible steam rising.

CHAPTER ONE

MEAT

PEANUT BUTTER BURGER WITH BACON & TOMATO CHILI JAM

A TWIST ON AMERICA'S FAVORITE SANDWICH, THIS UNIQUE BURGER IS THE PERFECT COMBINATION OF SWEET AND NOT-SO-SWEET.

PREP TIME: 10 MINUTES | COOK TIME: 30 MINUTES | SERVES: 4

1¾ pounds fresh ground beef

8 bacon strips

4 brioche burger buns, halved

8 large pickles, sliced

salt and pepper (optional)

TOMATO CHILI JAM

2 tablespoons olive oil

½ red onion, diced

1 garlic clove, crushed

½ teaspoon crushed red pepper flakes

2 tablespoons packed light brown sugar

1⅔ cups canned diced tomatoes

salt and pepper (optional)

PEANUT BUTTER SAUCE

2 tablespoons mayonnaise

¼ cup smooth peanut butter

1. Put the ground beef and salt and pepper, if using, into a large bowl. Using a wooden spoon, mix together, then shape into four equal patties. Press your thumb into the middle of each patty to help keep it an even size as it cooks. Set aside.

2. To make the jam, heat the oil in a medium saucepan over medium heat. Add the onions, garlic, and chile and cook for 5–8 minutes, until slightly golden, stirring frequently. Then add the sugar, tomatoes, salt, and pepper, if using. Cook for about 5 minutes, until the jam has reduced by half. Remove from the heat and let cool.

3. While the jam is cooking, vigorously whisk together the mayonnaise and peanut butter in a bowl to make the sauce, then set aside.

4. Heat a large nonstick skillet over medium heat, add the bacon strips, and slowly cook until crispy, turning every now and then. Once the bacon is cooked, remove and set aside.

5. Increase the heat, then add the patties to the large skillet and cook for 3 minutes on each side, until cooked to your preference.

6. Toast the brioche buns, then spread each side with the peanut butter sauce. Set a patty on top of each bottom half, then top with the jam, pickles, and crispy bacon. Serve immediately.

PER SERVING: 954 CAL | FAT: 54.6 G | SAT FAT: 18.9 G | CARBS: 56.3 G | SUGARS: 19.5 G | FIBER: 3.7 G | PROTEIN: 57.1 G | SODIUM: 960 MG

SPICY HAMBURGERS WITH GUACAMOLE

A HINT OF CHILE ADDS JUST A LITTLE HEAT TO THESE GROUND SIRLOIN BURGERS,
BUT YOU CAN ADD MORE SPICE TO SUIT YOUR TASTE.

PREP TIME: 30 MINUTES, PLUS CHILLING | COOK TIME: 10 MINUTES | SERVES: 4

1 pound 2 ounces sirloin steak, visible fat removed, diced

½ teaspoon chili powder

1 teaspoon cumin seeds, coarsely crushed

½ tablespoon fresh thyme leaves

1 tablespoon olive oil

4 seeded spelt rolls, halved

1 romaine lettuce heart, shredded

handful of arugula leaves (optional)

2 large tomatoes, sliced

salt and pepper (optional)

GUACAMOLE

1 large avocado, pitted and peeled

juice of 1 lime

2 scallions, finely chopped

salt and pepper (optional)

1. With the motor running on a food processor, drop in a few pieces of steak at a time until it has all been coarsely chopped. Alternatively, press the pieces through a grinder on the coarse setting.

2. Put the chili powder, cumin seeds, thyme, and a little salt and pepper, if using, into a bowl and mix well. Rub the seasonings into the steak, then shape the mixture into four patties. Cover and chill in the refrigerator for 15 minutes.

3. To make the guacamole, put the avocado into a shallow bowl and mash with a fork. Add the lime juice and scallions, season with a little salt and pepper, if using, and mix well.

4. Preheat the broiler to medium–high. Brush the patties with the oil, then cook, turning halfway through, for 8–10 minutes, or a little less for those who prefer their burgers pink in the middle. Let stand for a few minutes.

5. Meanwhile, toast the rolls, then top the bottom halves with lettuce, arugula, if using, and tomatoes, the hot patties, and a spoonful of guacamole and the roll lids. Serve immediately.

PER SERVING: 550 CAL | FAT: 28.7 G | SAT FAT: 6.7 G | CARBS: 36.6 G | SUGARS: 5.6 G | FIBER: 9.7 G | PROTEIN: 34.7 G | SODIUM: 320 MG

CHEESE & BACON BURGERS

THIS TRADITIONAL DINER FARE FEATURES THE HARD-TO-BEAT COMBINATION OF BEEF, BACON, AND CHEESE.

PREP TIME: 15 MINUTES | COOK TIME: 20 MINUTES | SERVES: 4

6 bacon strips

1 pound fresh chuck ground steak

4 cheddar cheese or American cheese slices

4 burger buns, halved

2 tablespoons mayonnaise

4 Boston lettuce leaves

2 large tomatoes, sliced

salt and pepper (optional)

1. Preheat the barbecue grill to medium–high. Put the bacon in a skillet over medium heat and cook for about 8 minutes, or until crisp. Drain on paper towels and break the strips in half.

2. Put the beef into a bowl and season with salt and pepper, if using. Divide into four equal portions and shape each portion into a patty.

3. Put the patties on the grate and cook, covered, for 4 minutes. Turn, top each patty with a slice of cheese, cover again, and cook for an additional 4 minutes, or until the burgers are cooked to your liking and the cheese is melted.

4. Spread both halves of the buns with mayonnaise, then place each burger on the bottom half of a bun. Top with the bacon pieces, lettuce, and tomato slices and finish with the top halves of the buns. Serve immediately.

PER SERVING: 553 CAL | FAT: 27.4 G | SAT FAT: 11.2 G | CARBS: 30.1 G | SUGARS: 4.3 G | FIBER: 3.6 G | PROTEIN: 43.5 G | SODIUM: 1,040 MG

DOUBLE-DECKER BURGERS

A DOUBLE-DECKER STACKS TWO BEEF PATTIES FOR A HUGE MOUTHFUL OF A BURGER.

PREP TIME: 20 MINUTES | COOK TIME: 10 MINUTES | SERVES: 4

2 pounds fresh ground chuck steak

1 teaspoon salt

½ teaspoon pepper

2 tablespoons olive oil, for brushing

8 cheddar cheese
or American cheese slices

4 burger buns, halved

4 Boston lettuce leaves

2 large tomatoes, sliced

1 red onion, sliced

8 pickles, halved lengthwise

1. Put the beef into a medium bowl with the salt and pepper and gently mix to combine. Divide into eight equal portions and shape each portion into a patty no thicker than ½ inch—the thinner the better for these burgers.

2. Put a large, ridged grill pan over medium–high heat. Lightly brush the patties with oil and cook for about 4 minutes, without moving, until the patties are brown and release easily from the pan. Turn and cook on the other side for 2 minutes, then put a slice of cheese on top of each patty and cook for an additional 2 minutes, or until cooked to your preference.

3. Put a patty on the bottom half of each bun, then place a second burger on top. Add the lettuce, tomato slices, onion slices, and pickles and serve immediately.

PER SERVING: 834 CAL | FAT: 47.5 G | SAT FAT: 20.3 G | CARBS: 34.4 G | SUGARS: 6.9 G | FIBER: 4.3 G | PROTEIN: 63 G | SODIUM: 1,440 MG

TRADITIONAL HAMBURGERS

NO BARBECUE IS COMPLETE WITHOUT THE TRADITIONAL HAMBURGER. THESE ARE SEASONED WITH ONION, GARLIC, AND MUSTARD, BUT YOU CAN MAKE THEM IN THE PURE TRADITION OF BEEF, SALT, AND PEPPER, IF YOU WANT.

PREP TIME: 15 MINUTES, PLUS CHILLING | COOK TIME: 20 MINUTES | SERVES: 4

1 pound lean chuck or sirloin steak, freshly ground

1 onion, grated

3 garlic cloves, crushed

2 teaspoons whole-grain mustard

1 teaspoon pepper

2 tablespoons sunflower oil, for brushing

4 soft burger buns, halved

¼ cup ketchup (optional)

FRIED ONIONS

2 tablespoons olive oil

3 onions (about 1 pound), finely sliced

2 teaspoons packed light brown sugar

1. Preheat the barbecue to medium–high. Place the ground beef, onion, garlic, mustard, and pepper into a large bowl and mix together thoroughly, squeezing the meat with your hand. Shape into four equal patties, then cover and let chill in the refrigerator for 30 minutes.

2. Meanwhile, make the fried onions. Heat the oil in a heavy skillet, add the onions, and sauté over low heat until soft. Add the sugar and cook for an additional 8 minutes, stirring occasionally, or until the onions have caramelized. Drain well on paper towels and keep warm.

3. To cook the burgers on the barbecue grill, check they are firm and brush generously with oil. Place them on the grate and cook for about 5 minutes on each side, or until cooked to your preference.

4. Cook the burger buns on the grate, cut side down, until lightly toasted. Place the burgers in the buns and top with the onions and ketchup, if using. Serve immediately.

PER SERVING: 532 CAL | FAT: 25.7 G | SAT FAT: 5.7 G | CARBS: 43.9 G | SUGARS: 10.8 G | FIBER: 5.3 G | PROTEIN: 29.7 G | SODIUM: 320 MG

TRADITIONAL CHEESEBURGERS

THERE IS SOMETHING ABOUT THE COMBINATION OF A JUICY HAMBURGER SIMPLY TOPPED WITH MELTED CHEESE THAT IS IRRESISTIBLY DELICIOUS.

PREP TIME: 10 MINUTES | COOK TIME: 10 MINUTES | SERVES: 4

1 pound 10 ounces fresh ground chuck steak

1 beef bouillon cube

1 tablespoon minced dried onion

2 tablespoons cold water

2 tablespoons sunflower oil, for brushing

½ cup shredded cheddar cheese or American cheese

4 Boston lettuce leaves

4 burger buns, halved

2 large tomatoes, sliced

1. Put the beef into a large mixing bowl. Crumble the bouillon cube over the meat, add the dried onion and water, and mix well. Divide the meat into four portions, shape each into a ball, then flatten slightly to make a patty of your preferred thickness.

2. Put a ridged grill pan over medium–high heat. Lightly brush the patties with oil and cook for 5–6 minutes. Turn the patties, sprinkle the cheese over the cooked side, and cook for an additional 5–6 minutes, or until cooked to your preference.

3. Put the lettuce on the bottom halves of the buns and top with the burgers. Place a couple of tomato slices on top and add the lids. Serve immediately.

PER SERVING: 608 CAL | FAT: 30.7 G | SAT FAT: 10.1 G | CARBS: 32 G | SUGARS: 4.9 G | FIBER: 3.9 G | PROTEIN: 47.4 G | SODIUM: 600 MG

THE EVERYTHING BURGER

THIS ALL-AMERICAN BURGER IS FILLED WITH COLORFUL LAYERS OF BACON, AVOCADO, JALAPEÑOS, AND COLESLAW.

PREP TIME: 30 MINUTES | COOK TIME: 20 MINUTES | SERVES: 4

4 bacon strips

1 pound fresh ground beef

1 tablespoon vegetable oil, for brushing

4 Monterey Jack cheese slices

¼ cup Dijon mustard

4 brioche buns, halved

pickled jalapeños (optional)

2 large tomatoes, sliced

4 Boston lettuce leaves

1 avocado, peeled and thinly sliced

salt and pepper (optional)

COLESLAW

1 cup shredded red cabbage

1½ cups shredded green cabbage

1½ cups shredded carrots

1 onion, finely sliced

2 red apples, such as Red Delicious, cored and chopped

¼ cup orange juice

2 celery stalks, finely sliced

¼ cup low-fat plain yogurt

1 tablespoon chopped fresh flat-leaf parsley

1. Put the bacon into a skillet over medium heat and cook for about 8 minutes, or until crisp. Drain on paper towels and break the strips in half.

2. Put the beef into a medium bowl with the salt and pepper, if using, and gently mix to combine. Divide into four equal portions and shape each portion into a patty.

3. Put a large skillet or ridged grill pan over medium–high heat. Lightly brush the patties with oil and add them to the pan. Partly cover and cook for about 4 minutes, without moving, until the patties are brown and release easily from the pan. Turn, place a slice of cheese on top of each patty, partly cover again, and cook for an additional 3 minutes, or until cooked to your preference.

4. To make the coleslaw, put the cabbage, carrots, and onion in a bowl and mix together. Toss the apples in the orange juice and add to the cabbage with any remaining orange juice and the celery. Mix well. Mix the yogurt and parsley in a bowl, then pour over the cabbage mixture and stir.

5. Spread the mustard on both halves of the buns and place a few slices of pickled jalapeños on the bottom half of each bun, if using, and set a patty on top. Then, layer on top of each patty the tomato slices, lettuce, bacon, coleslaw, and avocado slices. Serve immediately.

PER SERVING: 823 CAL | FAT: 41.4 G | SAT FAT: 17.7 G | CARBS: 68.8 G | SUGARS: 21.6 G | FIBER: 10.4 G | PROTEIN: 45.4 G | SODIUM: 1,000 MG

BARBECUE BURGERS

THIS SIMPLE HAMBURGER IS FLAVORED WITH ONION AND GARLIC AND TOPPED WITH A TASTY HOMEMADE BARBECUE SAUCE.

PREP TIME: 30 MINUTES | COOK TIME: 30 MINUTES | SERVES: 4

1 pound fresh ground chuck steak

½ small onion, finely sliced

1 garlic clove, finely chopped

4 soft burger buns, halved

4 Boston lettuce leaves

2 large tomatoes, sliced

salt and pepper (optional)

BARBECUE SAUCE

1 tablespoon olive oil

1 small onion, finely chopped

2 garlic cloves, crushed

1 fresh red jalapeño chile, seeded and finely chopped (optional)

2 teaspoons tomato paste

1 teaspoon dry mustard

1 tablespoon red wine vinegar

1 tablespoon Worcestershire sauce

1 tablespoon packed light brown sugar

1¼ cups cold water

1. To make the barbecue sauce, heat the oil in a small, heavy saucepan, add the onion, garlic, and chile, if using, and gently sauté, stirring frequently, for 3 minutes, or until beginning to soften.

2. Blend the tomato paste with the mustard, vinegar, and Worcestershire sauce into a paste, then stir into the onion mixture with 2 teaspoons of the sugar. Mix well, then gradually stir in the water.

3. Return to the heat and bring to a boil, stirring frequently. Reduce the heat and gently simmer, stirring occasionally, for 15 minutes. Taste and add the remaining sugar, if liked. Put ½ cup of the barbecue sauce into a bowl.

4. Preheat the barbecue grill to medium–high. Put the beef into a medium bowl with the salt and pepper, if using, onion and garlic and gently mix to combine. Divide into four equal portions and shape each portion into a patty.

5. Put the patties on the grate and cook for 4 minutes, until brown on one side. Turn, baste with the barbecue sauce, and cook for an additional 4 minutes, or until cooked to your preference.

6. Spread some of the remaining barbecue sauce on the buns, then place the patties in the buns. Top with the lettuce and tomato slices and serve immediately.

PER SERVING: 428 CAL | FAT: 16.4 G | SAT FAT: 5.1 G | CARBS: 38.9 G | SUGARS: 10.4 G | FIBER: 4.3 G | PROTEIN: 28.6 G | SODIUM: 320 MG

SLOPPY JOES

THE SECRET TO A GREAT SLOPPY JOE IS SLOWLY SIMMERING THE BEEF MIXTURE UNTIL IT'S RICH AND TENDER. YOU SHOULD ALWAYS SERVE SLOPPY JOES WITH A FORK, BUT YOU SHOULD NEVER NEED TO USE IT!

PREP TIME: 10 MINUTES | COOK TIME: 60 MINUTES | SERVES: 4

1½ pounds fresh lean ground beef

½ onion, diced

2 garlic cloves, finely chopped

1 green bell pepper, diced

2 cups cold water

¾ cup ketchup

1½ tablespoons packed light brown sugar

1 teaspoon Dijon mustard

1 teaspoon Worcestershire sauce

1 teaspoon salt

½ teaspoon black pepper

cayenne pepper (optional)

4 burger buns, halved

potato chips (optional)

1. Put the beef and onions into a cold large skillet and place over medium heat. Cook, stirring, breaking up the meat into small pieces with a wooden spoon, until it begins to brown.

2. Add the garlic and green bell pepper and cook, stirring, for 2 minutes. Add half the water. Cook until simmering, scraping up any sediment from the bottom of the pan.

3. Stir in the ketchup, sugar, mustard, Worcestershire sauce, salt, black pepper, cayenne pepper, if using, and the remaining water. Bring to simmering point, reduce the heat to low, and simmer for 30–45 minutes, or until most of the liquid has evaporated and the meat mixture is thick, rich, and tender.

4. Spoon the beef mixture onto the bottom half of each bun. Add the bun lids and serve immediately with potato chips, if using.

PER SERVING: 486 CAL | FAT: 13.2 G | SAT FAT: 5.1 G | CARBS: 48.8 G | SUGARS: 19.2 G | FIBER: 3.7 G | PROTEIN: 40.9 G | SODIUM: 1,360 MG

CHEESE-STUFFED BURGERS

YOU CAN CHOOSE ANY CHEESE YOU WANT FOR THIS RECIPE, BUT BE CAREFUL—THE MELTED FILLING WILL BE HOT WHEN THE BURGERS COME OFF THE BARBECUE.

PREP TIME: 20 MINUTES | COOK TIME: 25 MINUTES | SERVES: 2

11½ ounces fresh ground beef

½ teaspoon salt

½ teaspoon pepper

2 cheddar cheese or American cheese slices, quartered

1 tablespoon vegetable oil, for frying

½ red onion, sliced

2 soft burger buns, halved

4 Boston lettuce eaves

2 large tomatoes, sliced

1. Preheat the barbecue grill to medium–high. Put the beef into a small bowl with the salt and pepper and combine. Divide into four equal portions and roll each portion into a ball. Place the balls on a clean work surface and flatten until slightly larger than the buns and about ½ inch thick. Arrange the cheese on top of two of the patties, leaving a ½-inch border. Add the remaining two patties and firmly press the sides together to seal (otherwise the cheese will come out during cooking).

2. Heat the oil in a skillet over medium heat. Add the onion slices and sauté for about 8 minutes, stirring frequently, until soft and brown. Alternatively, you could barbecue the onion slices for about 2 minutes on each side while you cook the patties.

3. Put the patties on the grated, rounded side up. Cook for 8 minutes, then carefully turn over and cook on the other side for 5–7 minutes.

4. Put each burger on the bottom halve of a bun, top with the onions, lettuce, tomatoes, and the top half of the bun, and serve immediately.

PER SERVING: 629 CAL | FAT: 33.1 G | SAT FAT: 12.5 G | CARBS: 35.6 G | SUGARS: 7 G | FIBER: 5.2 G | PROTEIN: 44.9 G | SODIUM: 1,080 MG

BLACK & BLUE BURGERS

THESE BURGERS GET THEIR NAME FROM A BLACK PEPPER SPICE RUB AND A BLUE CHEESE DRESSING.

PREP TIME: 30 MINUTES | COOK TIME: 10 MINUTES | SERVES: 4

1 pound fresh ground beef

4 burger buns, halved

4 Boston lettuce leaves

2 large tomatoes, sliced

BLUE CHEESE DRESSING

1 cup crumbled blue cheese

¼ cup mayonnaise

¼ cup sour cream

1 shallot, finely chopped

SPICE RUB

1 teaspoon pepper

1 teaspoon paprika

1 teaspoon dried thyme

1 teaspoon salt

½ teaspoon cayenne pepper

1. To make the blue cheese dressing, put the cheese, mayonnaise, and sour cream into a bowl and mash together until the mixture is as smooth as possible. Add the shallot and stir it into the dressing. Set aside.

2. To make the spice rub, mix the black pepper, paprika, thyme, salt, and cayenne pepper together in a small bowl.

3. Divide the beef into four equal portions and shape each portion into a patty. Sprinkle evenly on both sides with the spice rub.

4. Heat a large, nonstick skillet over high heat. Add the patties and cook for about 4 minutes, until the spice mixture forms a light crust and the edges are brown. Turn and cook on the other side for an additional 4 minutes, until brown and cooked to your preference.

5. Transfer the burgers to the buns, top with the blue cheese dressing, lettuce, and tomato slices, and serve immediately.

PER SERVING: 577 CAL | FAT: 32.9 G | SAT FAT: 12.7 G | CARBS: 33.4 G | SUGARS: 5.2 G | FIBER: 4.2 G | PROTEIN: 34.7 G | SODIUM: 1,320 MG

STEAKHOUSE BURGERS

THE ULTIMATE BEST BURGERS ARE MADE WITH FRESHLY CHOPPED MEAT, AND YOU DON'T NEED A MEAT GRINDER FOR THE TASK.

PREP TIME: 20 MINUTES, PLUS CHILLING | COOK TIME: 10 MINUTES | SERVES: 4

1 pound chuck steak or a mixture with at least 20 percent fat

1 teaspoon salt

½ teaspoon pepper

4 Gruyère cheese slices

2 tablespoons mayonnaise

2 tablespoons ketchup

4 burger buns, halved

4 Boston lettuce leaves

2 large tomatoes, sliced

1. Preheat the barbecue grill to medium–high. Chop the steak into 1-inch cubes, then put onto a plate, wrap in plastic wrap, and chill in the refrigerator for about 30 minutes.

2. Put half the steak into a food processor or blender. Pulse (do not run the processor) about 15 times. Season the meat with half the salt and half the pepper, and pulse an additional 10–15 times, until the meat is finely chopped but not overprocessed. Remove from the processor and repeat with the remaining beef. Divide into four equal portions and shape each portion into a patty.

3. Put the patties on the grate and cook until cooked to your preference: 3 minutes on each side for medium–rare and 4 minutes on each side for medium. Place a slice of cheese on each patty during the last 2 minutes of cooking.

4. Meanwhile, put the mayonnaise and ketchup into a small bowl and mix to combine. Spread on the buns, then add the patties with the lettuce and tomato slices. Serve immediately.

PER SERVING: 639 CAL | FAT: 40.6 G | SAT FAT: 18.4 G | CARBS: 32.7 G | SUGARS: 6.2 G | FIBER: 3.7 G | PROTEIN: 34.6 G | SODIUM: 1,200 MG

SMOKED BURGERS

SMOKED GOUDA CHEESE ADDS EXTRA FLAVOR TO THESE LIGHTLY SMOKED HAMBURGERS,
AND A SWEET PLUM RELISH MAKES A DELICIOUS ACCOMPANIMENT.

PREP TIME: 15 MINUTES | COOK TIME: 10 MINUTES | SERVES: 4

wood chips, for smoking
1 pound fresh ground beef
4 smoked Gouda cheese slices
4 brioche buns, halved
¼ cup plum relish
salt and pepper (optional)

1. Soak the wood chips in water for at least 10 minutes.

2. Put the beef into a bowl with the salt and pepper, if using, and gently mix to combine. Divide into four equal portions and shape each portion into a patty.

3. If using a gas barbecue grill, wrap the drained wood chips in aluminum foil, making a pouch but leaving the ends open to let the smoke escape. Lift the grate, place the pouch on top of a side burner, and turn the heat to high. Turn the other burners to medium or low, cover, and preheat the barbecue to 400°F.

4. If using a charcoal barbecue grill, preheat to medium–high. Push the coals to one side and place the wood chips on top.

5. When the wood starts smoking, place the patties on the grate on the opposite side of the grill. Cover and cook for about 4 minutes, until brown, then turn and cook on the other side. After 2 minutes, add the cheese and cook for an additional 2 minutes, or until the patties are brown and cooked to your preference.

6. Put the burgers in the buns and top with some of the relish. Serve immediately.

PER SERVING: 571 CAL | FAT: 26.9 G | SAT FAT: 14.4 G | CARBS: 44.7 G | SUGARS: 10 G | FIBER: 2.3 G | PROTEIN: 35.2 G | SODIUM: 720 MG

PORCINI BURGERS

DRIED PORCINI ARE GROUND TO A POWDER, SO THE MUSHROOMS CAN DELICATELY PERFUME AND SEASON THE MEAT IN THESE BURGERS.

PREP TIME: 10 MINUTES | COOK TIME: 10 MINUTES | SERVES: 4

1 ounce dried porcini

2 tablespoons olive oil, plus extra for grilling

1 teaspoon salt

½ teaspoon pepper

1 pound fresh ground beef

½ cup shredded Gruyère cheese,

4 brioche buns, halved

4 teaspoons butter, softened

caramelized red onion chutney (optional)

1. Grind the mushrooms to a powder in a spice grinder or clean coffee grinder. You should have about 2 tablespoons. Put the powder into a bowl with the oil, salt, and pepper and stir until the salt is dissolved. If necessary, add up to 2 teaspoons of water to thin the mixture. Add the beef and gently mix to combine, then divide into four equal portions and form each portion into a patty.

2. Heat a ridged grill pan over medium–high heat, then coat with the oil. Place the patties in the pan and cover. Cook for about 4 minutes on each side, until browned. Turn over, and after 2 minutes, put the cheese on top of the patties and cook for an additional 2 minutes, until the burgers are browned and cooked to your preference.

3. Spread the buns with butter and place the burgers in the buns. Top with the onion chutney, if using, and serve immediately.

PER SERVING: 655 CAL | FAT: 38 G | SAT FAT: 16.1 G | CARBS: 40.8 G | SUGARS: 5.4 G | FIBER: 3.2 G | PROTEIN: 34.7 G | SODIUM: 1,000 MG

AUSTRALIAN BURGERS

A TRADITIONAL AUSTRALIAN COMBINATION OF BEETS, GRILLED PINEAPPLE, AND A FRIED EGG MAKE THIS MILE-HIGH BURGER EXTRA-SATISFYING.

PREP TIME: 20 MINUTES | COOK TIME: 18 MINUTES | SERVES: 4

1 pound fresh ground beef

3 tablespoons vegetable oil, for brushing and frying

4 pineapple slices

4 eggs

4 soft burger buns, halved

¼ cup mayonnaise

8 beet slices in vinegar

4 Boston lettuce leaves

2 large tomatoes, sliced

salt and pepper (optional)

1. Put the beef into a medium bowl with salt and pepper, if using. Mix gently to combine, then divide into four equal portions and shape each portion into a patty.

2. Put a ridged grill pan over medium–high heat and add 1 tablespoon of the oil. Lightly brush the patties and pineapple slices with 1 tablespoon of oil and place the patties and pineapple in the pan. Cover and cook the pineapple for 3 minutes on each side, until each slice is soft and marked, and cook the patties for about 4 minutes on each side, until brown and cooked to your preference. Remove from the heat and keep warm.

3. Add 1 tablespoon of oil to a skillet, swirling to coat the pan. Add the eggs and season with salt and pepper, if using. Cover and cook for about 3 minutes, until the whites are set and the yolks are beginning to set at the edges.

4. Spread some mayonnaise on each half of the buns. Place a pineapple slice and a lettuce leaf on the bottom half of each bun, then add a patty, two beet slices, tomato slices, and an egg. Finish with the bun tops and serve immediately.

PER SERVING: 663 CAL | FAT: 38 G | SAT FAT: 8.8 G | CARBS: 42.4 G | SUGARS: 12.8 G | FIBER: 4.9 G | PROTEIN: 34.9 G | SODIUM: 520 MG

BEEF TERIYAKI BURGERS

TERIYAKI SAUCE IS USED AS A MARINADE TO TENDERIZE THE BEEF
AND INFUSE IT WITH SOME ASIAN FLAVORS.

PREP TIME: 10 MINUTES, PLUS CHILLING | COOK TIME: 10 MINUTES | SERVES: 4

1 pound fresh ground beef

8 scallions, chopped

4 garlic cloves, chopped

1-inch piece fresh ginger, grated

½ teaspoon wasabi paste

1 tablespoon teriyaki sauce or teriyaki marinade

2 tablespoons peanut oil

1 cup shredded carrot

1⅔ cups shredded bok choy

⅙ cucumber, shredded

4 burger buns, halved

crispy fried seaweed, to garnish (optional)

1. Put the ground beef, scallions, garlic, ginger, wasabi, and teriyaki sauce into a food processor or blender and, using the pulse button, blend together. Shape into four equal patties, then cover and let chill in the refrigerator for 30 minutes.

2. Heat a heavy skillet over medium–high heat and add 1 tablespoon of the oil. When hot, add the patties and cook over medium heat for 3–5 minutes on each side, or until cooked to your preference. Keep warm.

3. Put the carrot, bok choy, cucumber, and the remaining oil into a small bowl and mix together.

4. Spoon a little of the vegetables onto the bottom half of each bun and top with the burgers and seaweed, if using. Add the bun lids and serve immediately.

PER SERVING: 444 CAL | FAT: 18.9 G | SAT FAT: 5.3 G | CARBS: 36.7 G | SUGARS: 7 G | FIBER: 4.7 G | PROTEIN: 29.5 G | SODIUM: 440 MG

CHILI-GARLIC SAUCE BURGERS

A MIXTURE OF BEEF AND GROUND PORK ADDS A DISTINCTIVE FLAVOR TO THESE BURGERS, AND THE CHILI-GARLIC SAUCE PACKS A REAL PUNCH.

PREP TIME: 20 MINUTES, PLUS CHILLING | COOK TIME: 20 MINUTES | SERVES: 4

⅔ cup fresh cilantro

1 garlic clove, finely chopped

8 ounces fresh ground beef

8 ounces fresh ground pork

2 tablespoons red chili sauce

2 teaspoons fresh ginger, finely grated

2 teaspoons soy sauce

2 small bok choy

2 teaspoons vegetable oil

4 burger buns, halved

1. Finely chop half of the cilantro leaves and put into a large bowl with the garlic, beef, pork, chili sauce, ginger, and soy sauce and mix to combine. Divide the mixture into four equal portions and shape each portion into a ½–¾-inch-thick patty. Cover and chill in the refrigerator for 30 minutes.

2. Coarsely chop the bok choy, discarding the thick ends. Put a large skillet over high heat and add the oil, swirling to cover the bottom of the pan. Add the bok choy and cook, stirring frequently, until wilted. Set aside.

3. Put the patties in the skillet and cook for about 4 minutes, until brown. Turn and cook for an additional 4 minutes, until they are cooked through and brown on both sides.

4. Put a patty on the bottom half of each bun. Top with some sautéed bok choy, the whole cilantro leaves, and the top halves of the buns. Serve immediately.

PER SERVING: 427 CAL | FAT: 21.3 G | SAT FAT: 7 G | CARBS: 30.1 G | SUGARS: 3.8 G | FIBER: 3.6 G | PROTEIN: 26.6 G | SODIUM: 520 MG

COFFEE BURGERS

COFFEE ADDS A PUNCH OF FLAVOR TO THESE HAMBURGERS, AS WELL AS A HIT OF CAFFEINE.

PREP TIME: 15 MINUTES | COOK TIME: 20 MINUTES | SERVES: 4

1 tablespoon instant coffee granules, finely ground

2 teaspoons packed light brown sugar

1 teaspoon salt

¼ teaspoon pepper

1 pound 2 ounces fresh ground beef

1 small onion, grated

1 egg yolk

1 tablespoon olive oil, for brushing

4 soft burger buns, halved

¼ cup mayonnaise

1 teaspoon smooth mustard

3½ cups peppery salad greens

2 large tomatoes, sliced

1. Put the coffee, sugar, salt, and pepper into a large bowl and mix together. Add the beef, onion, and egg yolk and mix together with your hands until thoroughly combined. Divide the mixture into four portions and shape each portion into a patty.

2. Preheat a ridged grill pan or cast-iron skillet to medium–high. Lightly brush the patties with oil and cook for 6–8 minutes on each side, or until cooked through. Alternatively, cook under a hot broiler.

3. To serve, lightly toast the burger buns. Mix the mayonnaise and mustard together. Put some salad greens, tomato slices, and a patty on top of four bun halves. Add a dollop of mustard mayonnaise and top with the remaining bun halves. Serve immediately.

PER SERVING: 543 CAL | FAT: 28.5 G | SAT FAT: 7.6 G | CARBS: 36.2 G | SUGARS: 8.2 G | FIBER: 4.2 G | PROTEIN: 32 G | SODIUM: 1,000 MG

TURKISH LAMB BURGERS WITH EGGPLANT

THESE LIGHTLY SPICED BURGERS, SERVED BETWEEN THICK, MEATY SLICES OF EGGPLANT WITH A SIDE OF A TRADITIONAL TURKISH-STYLE SAUCE, WILL HAVE YOU COMING BACK TO THIS RECIPE TIME AND AGAIN.

PREP TIME: 15 MINUTES | COOK TIME: 20 MINUTES | SERVES: 2

8 ounces fresh ground lamb

2 garlic cloves, crushed

1 teaspoon ground cumin

1 teaspoon sumac

1 medium egg, beaten

1½ tablespoons olive oil

½ large red bell pepper, seeded and quartered

1 small onion, thinly sliced into rings

4 large round eggplant slices, each ½–¾ inch thick

2 teaspoons olive oil, for brushing

salt and pepper (optional)

2 frisée lettuce leaves, to serve

TURKISH-STYLE SAUCE

4-inch piece cucumber

3 tablespoons thick plain Greek-style yogurt

2 teaspoons chopped fresh dill

1 teaspoon white wine vinegar

¼ teaspoon salt

1. Add the lamb, half the garlic, all the cumin, sumac, egg, and salt and pepper, if using, to a bowl. Combine well and shape into two thick patties. Set aside.

2. Heat 1 tablespoon of the oil in a nonstick skillet over medium–high heat. Add the red bell pepper and onion rings and cook for 3–4 minutes, until soft and slightly charred all over. Transfer to a warm plate with a slotted spoon. Add the eggplant slices to the pan with the remaining oil and cook for 2–3 minutes on each side, until slightly soft and brown. Transfer to the plate with the red pepper and onion and season with salt and pepper, if using.

3. To make the Turkish-style sauce, cut the cucumber in half lengthwise and seed. Lightly peel, leaving some green skin, then finely chop. Put onto a clean dish towel, wrap, and squeeze out as much of the juice as possible. Put the cucumber into a bowl with the yogurt, the remaining garlic, and the dill, vinegar, and salt.

4. Brush the pan with oil and heat until hot. Add the lamb patties and cook, without moving around, for 4–5 minutes on each side, or until cooked through.

5. To assemble each burger, put a slice of eggplant on a serving plate, top with a lettuce leaf, a red bell pepper slice, and a little onion, followed by the lamb burger. Add the remaining red bell pepper and onion slices, then add a spoonful of the Turkish-style sauce. Top with another eggplant slice. Serve the remaining sauce on the side.

PER SERVING: 549 CAL | FAT: 40.9 G | SAT FAT: 15 G | CARBS: 15.4 G | SUGARS: 7.5 G | FIBER: 4.1 G | PROTEIN: 31.3 G | SODIUM: 440 MG

LAMB BURGERS WITH TZATZIKI & FETA

THESE LAMB BURGERS ARE DELICIOUS, AND THE HERBED GREEK YOGURT SAUCE KNOWN AS TZATZIKI, TANGY PICKLED ONIONS, AND SALTY FETA CHEESE ARE THE PERFECT ACCOMPANIMENTS.

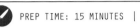 PREP TIME: 15 MINUTES | COOK TIME: 10 MINUTES | SERVES: 4

1 pound 2 ounces fresh ground lamb

1 teaspoon cumin seeds

1 tablespoon vegetable oil, for brushing

4 burger buns, halved

⅔ cup crumbled feta cheese

salt and pepper (optional)

TZATZIKI

¼ cup Greek-style yogurt

⅔ cup chopped fresh mint

½ cup chopped fresh dill

½ cucumber, sliced

salt and pepper (optional)

PICKLED ONIONS

1 red onion, sliced

2 tablespoons red wine vinegar

½ teaspoon salt

1. Preheat the barbecue grill to medium–high and brush the grate with a little oil. To make the patties, mix the lamb, cumin seeds, and salt and pepper, if using, together in a medium bowl.

2. Divide the mixture into four equal balls, then shape into patties.

3. To make the tzatziki, mix all of the ingredients together in a small bowl and stir to combine.

4. To make the pickled onions, mix the onion, vinegar, and salt together in a separate small bowl.

5. Cook the patties on the grill for 5 minutes on each side, or until cooked through.

6. Divide the patties among the buns and top with the tzatziki, feta cheese, and pickled onions. Serve immediately.

PER SERVING: 623 CAL | FAT: 36.1 G | SAT FAT: 17.6 G | CARBS: 35.4 G | SUGARS: 6.6 G | FIBER: 4.1 G | PROTEIN: 37.7 G | SODIUM: 920 MG

HERBED LAMB BURGERS

SOMETIMES, THE SIMPLICITY OF FRESH HERBS IS ALL YOU NEED TO MIX WITH LAMB TO CREATE A FLAVORSOME BURGER.

PREP TIME: 10 MINUTES | COOK TIME: 8 MINUTES | SERVES: 4

1 pound fresh lean ground lamb

1⅔ cups fresh bread crumbs

1 onion, finely chopped

3 tablespoons chopped fresh herbs, such as mint, rosemary, or thyme

1 egg, beaten

½ tablespoon apple juice

2 tablespoons vegetable oil

4 Boston lettuce leaves

4 burger buns, halved

2 large tomatoes, sliced

salt and pepper (optional)

1. Put the lamb into a large mixing bowl. Add the bread crumbs, onion, chopped herbs, egg, and apple juice. Season with salt and pepper, if using, and mix together.

2. Divide the mixture into four equal portions, shape each portion into a ball, then flatten slightly to make a patty shape of your preferred thickness.

3. Put a large skillet over medium–high heat and add the oil. When hot, add the patties and cook for 3–4 minutes on each side, until cooked through.

4. Place the lettuce on the bottom halves of the buns and top with the tomato slices. Place the burgers on top and add the lids. Serve immediately.

PER SERVING: 603 CAL | FAT: 32.6 G | SAT FAT: 12.9 G | CARBS: 42.4 G | SUGARS: 6.7 G | FIBER: 4.9 G | PROTEIN: 33.2 G | SODIUM: 480 MG

MOROCCAN LAMB BURGERS

THESE BURGERS GET THEIR DISTINCTIVE FLAVOR FROM
AN AROMATIC BLEND OF SPICES AND SPICY HARISSA SAUCE.

PREP TIME: 20 MINUTES, PLUS STANDING | COOK TIME: 12 MINUTES | SERVES: 4

1¼ pounds fresh ground lamb

1 onion, finely chopped

1 teaspoon harissa sauce

1 garlic clove, crushed

2 tablespoons chopped fresh mint

½ teaspoon cumin seeds, crushed

½ teaspoon paprika

2 tablespoons olive oil, for brushing

4 pita breads, warmed and halved

½ red onion, sliced

salt and pepper (optional)

handful of arugula leaves
(optional)

YOGURT & CUCUMBER SAUCE

½ large cucumber

1 teaspoon salt

¼ cup plain yogurt

6 tablespoons chopped fresh mint

1. Preheat the barbecue to medium–high. To make the sauce, peel the cucumber, quarter it lengthwise, and scoop out the seeds. Chop the flesh and put into a strainer set over a bowl. Sprinkle with salt, cover with a plate, and weigh down with a can of vegetables. Let drain for 30 minutes, then mix with the remaining ingredients.

2. Meanwhile, combine the lamb, onion, harissa sauce, garlic, mint, cumin seeds, and paprika. Season with salt and pepper, if using, mixing well with a fork. Divide into four equal portions and flatten into patties about 1 inch thick. Cover and let stand at room temperature for 30 minutes.

3. Lightly brush the patties with oil. Grease the grate. Cook for 5–6 minutes on each side, or until cooked through.

4. Stuff the burgers into the pita breads with the red onion slices, arugula leaves, if using, and a spoonful of the sauce. Serve immediately.

PER SERVING: 642 CAL | FAT: 36.1 G | SAT FAT: 15.4 G | CARBS: 41.2 G | SUGARS: 4.6 G | FIBER: 3.3 G | PROTEIN: 36.9 G | SODIUM: 1,080 MG

PORK BELLY SLIDERS
WITH KIMCHI SLAW

SLIDERS ARE SMALL BURGERS AND ARE GREAT TO SERVE AT A DINNER PARTY.
THESE JAPANESE-INSPIRED PORK BELLY SLIDERS MIGHT BE SMALL IN SIZE, BUT THEY'RE BIG ON FLAVOR.

PREP TIME: 20 MINUTES | COOK TIME: 2 HOURS 15 MINUTES | MAKES: 14

2¼ pounds pork belly

3 star anise or 1½ teaspoons five-spice powder

1 cinnamon stick

5 dried shiitake mushrooms

5 scallions

1 cup sugar

½ cup light soy sauce

1¼ cups rice wine

½ cup rice vinegar

14 slider buns, halved

6 tablespoons Japanese mayonnaise, for spreading

KIMCHI SLAW

3 tablespoons Japanese mayonnaise

½ green cabbage, finely sliced

1 cup sliced kimchi,

4 scallions, sliced

4 teaspoons chopped pickled ginger

1. Preheat the oven to 350°F.

2. Place the pork belly, star anise, cinnamon stick, mushrooms, scallions, sugar, soy sauce, rice wine, and rice vinegar into a baking dish. Cover with wax paper and aluminum foil.

3. Roast in the preheated oven for 2 hours, or until the center of the meat is no longer pink and the juices run clear when the thickest part of the meat is pierced with the tip of a sharp knife. Let cool completely in the cooking liquid.

4. To make the slaw, mix all the ingredients together in a medium bowl.

5. Preheat the barbecue grill to medium–high. Slice the pork into ¾-inch-thick slices. Place the slices on the grate and cook for 3–4 minutes on each side, or until starting to caramelize.

6. Cut the pork slices into squares. Spread each bun half with mayonnaise, then fill with the pork squares and top with slaw.

PER SERVING: 415 CAL | FAT: 34.3 G | SAT FAT: 10.7 G | CARBS: 19.1 G | SUGARS: 5 G | FIBER: 1.1 G | PROTEIN: 11.8 G | SODIUM: 320 MG

BARBECUED CAJUN PORK BURGERS

**THE CAJUN SEASONING REALLY LIVENS UP THE FLAVOR
OF THESE PORK BURGERS, AND GRATED APPLE KEEPS THEM JUICY.**

PREP TIME: 20 MINUTES, PLUS CHILLING | COOK TIME: 35–40 MINUTES | SERVES: 4

1 teaspoon salt

1 large sweet potato,
cut into chunks

1 pound fresh ground pork

1 apple, peeled, cored, and grated

2 teaspoons Cajun seasoning

2 onions

1 tablespoon chopped
fresh cilantro

2 tablespoons sunflower oil

8 bacon strips

salt and pepper (optional)

1. Bring a saucepan of lightly salted water to a boil, add the sweet potato, and cook for 15–20 minutes, or until soft when pierced with a fork. Drain well, then mash and reserve.

2. Put the pork into a bowl, add the mashed sweet potato, apple, and Cajun seasoning. Grate one of the onions and add to the pork mixture with the cilantro, and salt and pepper, if using. Mix together, then shape into four equal patties. Cover and chill in the refrigerator for 1 hour.

3. Slice the remaining onion. Heat 1 tablespoon of the oil in a skillet. Add the sliced onion and cook over low heat for 10–12 minutes, stirring until soft. Remove the pan from the heat and reserve. Wrap each patty in two bacon strips.

4. Preheat the barbecue grill to medium–high. Brush the patties with the remaining oil and cook for 4–5 minutes on each side, or until thoroughly cooked. Serve immediately with the fried onions.

PER SERVING: 547 CAL | FAT: 36.9 G | SAT FAT: 11.9 G | CARBS: 21.2 G | SUGARS: 7.8 G | FIBER: 3.3 G | PROTEIN: 32 G | SODIUM: 1,080 MG

SPICY PULLED PORK BURGERS

TENDER, MOIST, AND FLAVORED WITH A BARBECUE-STYLE SAUCE,
THIS SHREDDED PORK IS COOKED FOR 8 HOURS IN A SLOW COOKER.

PREP TIME: 20 MINUTES | COOK TIME: 8 HOURS | SERVES: 6

2 onions, sliced

3 pounds 5 ounces boned and rolled pork shoulder

2 tablespoons raw brown sugar

2 tablespoons Worcestershire sauce

1 tablespoon yellow mustard

2 tablespoons ketchup

1 tablespoon apple cider vinegar

4 burger buns, halved

salt and pepper (optional)

1. Put the onions into the slow cooker and place the pork on top. Mix together the sugar, Worcestershire sauce, mustard, ketchup, and vinegar and spread all over the surface of the pork. Season with salt and pepper, if using. Cover and cook on low for 8 hours.

2. Remove the pork from the slow cooker and use two forks to pull it apart into shreds.

3. Skim any excess fat from the juices and stir a little juice into the shredded pork. Serve in burger buns, with the remaining juices for spooning over the top.

PER SERVING: 651 CAL | FAT: 18 G | SAT FAT: 5.4 G | CARBS: 39.2 G | SUGARS: 11.8 G | FIBER: 2.3 G | PROTEIN: 82.2 G | SODIUM: 600 MG

PORK & ORANGE BURGERS

THE PIQUANT FLAVOR OF ORANGE JUICE AND ZEST IS THE MAKING OF THIS BURGER, AND THE ORANGE PEEL IN THE MARMALADE ADDS EXTRA TEXTURE.

🔪 PREP TIME: 45 MINUTES, PLUS CHILLING | 🔥 COOK TIME: 45 MINUTES | 🍔 SERVES: 4

1 pound pork tenderloin, cut into small pieces

2 parsnips, cut into chunks

1 tablespoon finely grated orange zest

2 garlic cloves, crushed

6 scallions, finely chopped

1 zucchini, shredded

1 tablespoon sunflower oil

4 Boston lettuce leaves

4 burger buns, halved

salt and pepper (optional)

ORANGE MARINADE

3 tablespoons Seville orange marmalade

2 tablespoons orange juice

1 tablespoon balsamic vinegar

1. To make the marinade, put the marmalade, orange juice, and vinegar into a small saucepan and heat, stirring, until the marmalade is runny. Put the pork into a shallow dish and pour the marinade over it. Cover and let rest for at least 30 minutes. Remove the pork, reserving the marinade. Mince the pork pieces in a large bowl.

2. Meanwhile, cook the parsnips in a saucepan of boiling water for 15–20 minutes, or until tender. Drain, then mash and add to the pork. Stir in the orange zest, garlic, scallions, zucchini, and salt and pepper, if using. Mix together, then shape into four equal burgers. Cover and let chill in the refrigerator for at least 30 minutes.

3. Preheat the barbecue grill to medium–high. Lightly brush each patty with the oil, then add them to the grate and cook for 4–6 minutes on each side, or until cooked through. Boil the reserved marinade for at least 5 minutes, then pour into a small pitcher or bowl.

4. Place the lettuce on the bottom halves of the burger buns and top with the burgers. Spoon over a little of the hot marinade, then top with the lids and serve immediately.

PER SERVING: 438 CAL | FAT: 11.2 G | SAT FAT: 2.7 G | CARBS: 53.7 G | SUGARS: 17.7 G | FIBER: 7.1 G | PROTEIN: 29.8 G | SODIUM: 320 MG

BANH MI-STYLE BURGERS

INSPIRED BY VIETNAMESE SANDWICHES, THESE FRAGRANT BURGERS ARE PREPARED
WITH FIVE-SPICE POWDER AND THEN STUFFED INTO BURGER BUNS WITH PICKLED VEGETABLES.

PREP TIME: 30 MINUTES, PLUS MARINATING | COOK TIME: 10 MINUTES | SERVES: 4

1 pound fresh ground pork

1 garlic clove, finely chopped

1 tablespoon Thai fish sauce

1 teaspoon five-spice powder

½ teaspoon sugar

¼ teaspoon pepper

¼ cup mayonnaise

4 burger buns, halved

½ cucumber, thinly sliced

1 fresh jalapeño chile, thinly sliced

6–8 fresh cilantro sprigs

2 tablespoons soy sauce

PICKLED VEGETABLES

2 large carrots, cut into julienne strips

½ daikon, cut into julienne strips

1 teaspoon sugar

¾ cup distilled white vinegar

¾ cup water

1 teaspoon salt (optional)

1. To make the pickled vegetables, put the carrots and daikon into a medium bowl and toss with the sugar and salt, if using. Add the vinegar and water and marinate in the refrigerator for at least 30 minutes or overnight.

2. Put the pork, garlic, fish sauce, five-spice powder, sugar, and pepper into a medium bowl and combine. Stir gently, then divide into four equal portions and shape each portion into a patty.

3. Place a ridged grill pan over medium–high heat, add the patties, and cook for 5 minutes on each side, until brown and cooked through.

4. Spread the mayonnaise on the buns and stuff each with a burger, cucumber slices, and a few chile slices. Top with some pickled vegetables and cilantro. Drizzle with soy sauce and serve immediately.

PER SERVING: 590 CAL | FAT: 34.7 G | SAT FAT: 10.5 G | CARBS: 39.8 G | SUGARS: 9.7 G | FIBER: 5.3 G | PROTEIN: 25.9 G | SODIUM: 1,280 MG

CHAPTER TWO

POULTRY

TURMERIC CHICKEN BURGER WITH TANDOORI MAYO

AN INDIAN-INSPIRED CHICKEN BURGER ACCOMPANIED BY A LIGHT AND MILDLY SPICED SLAW.

PREP TIME: 10 MINUTES, PLUS MARINADE | COOK TIME: 20 MINUTES | SERVES: 4

2 tablespoons vegetable oil

1 teaspoon grated ginger

1 teaspoon crushed garlic

½ teaspoon turmeric powder

4 chicken breasts, skin removed

4 burger buns, halved

salt and pepper (optional)

TANDOORI MAYONNAISE

6 tablespoons mayonnaise

1 tablespoon tandoori masala powder

1 tablespoon lemon juice

COLESLAW

½ red onion, finely sliced

½ cup finely sliced green cabbage

½ cup finely sliced red cabbaged

1 small carrot, finely sliced

¼ cup fresh cilantro leaves

⅓ cup grated coconut flesh

½ teaspoon cumin seeds

1. In a large bowl, mix together the oil, ginger, garlic, turmeric powder, and salt and pepper, if using, to make a marinade. Add the chicken breasts and mix together, then cover with plastic wrap and refrigerate for 2 hours.

2. To make the tandoori mayonnaise, mix together the mayonnaise, tandoori powder, and lemon juice in a small bowl.

3. To make the coleslaw, mix together all the ingredients in a medium bowl.

4. Preheat a large, ridged grill pan to medium–high. Remove the chicken from the refrigerator and drain off the excess marinade.

5. Once the ridged grill pan is hot, add the chicken breasts and cook for 8 minutes on each side, or until thoroughly cooked; there should be no traces of pink when cutting through the thickest part of the meat.

6. Toast the burger buns, then spread with the tandoori mayonnaise.

7. Place a chicken breast on the bottom half of each bun and top with the coleslaw and bun lid. Serve immediately.

PER SERVING: 544 CAL | FAT: 28.1 G | SAT FAT: 5.9 G | CARBS: 35.4 G | SUGARS: 5.7 G | FIBER: 5.5 G | PROTEIN: 34.9 G | SODIUM: 440 MG

BUTTERMILK CHICKEN BURGERS WITH SPICY SLAW

CRISPY BUTTERMILK CHICKEN BURGERS AND CRUNCHY, CREAMY, SPICY COLESLAW ARE A MATCH MADE IN HEAVEN.

PREP TIME: 20 MINUTES | COOK TIME: 6 MINUTES | SERVES: 4

4 chicken breasts, each about ½ inch thick

1 cup buttermilk

1 cup all-purpose flour

1 tablespoon smoked paprika

2 teaspoons garlic powder

½ teaspoon cayenne pepper

½ cup vegetable oil

¼ cup mayonnaise

4 burger buns, halved

2 large tomatoes, sliced

4 Boston lettuce leaves

salt and pepper (optional)

SPICY SLAW

½ cup wine vinegar

½ cup mayonnaise

2 tablespoons sour cream

2 tablespoons sugar

¾ teaspoon salt

1 teaspoon hot sauce

½ teaspoon pepper

¼ teaspoon cayenne pepper

½ red onion, thinly sliced

1 cup shredded red cabbage

1 cup shredded green cabbage

2 carrots, shredded

1. Put the chicken breasts into a bowl with the buttermilk and toss to coat. Set aside.

2. To make the spicy slaw, combine the vinegar, mayonnaise, sour cream, sugar, salt, hot sauce, pepper, and cayenne pepper. Add the onion, cabbage, and carrot to the dressing and toss to coat.

3. Put the flour into a shallow bowl and add the paprika, garlic powder, cayenne pepper, and salt and pepper, if using. Stir to mix. Remove the chicken breasts, one at a time, from the buttermilk and dip them in the flour mixture. Return to the buttermilk and dip again in the flour mixture. Heat the oil in a large skillet over medium–high heat until hot. Add the chicken in a single layer and cook for about 3 minutes on each side, until golden brown and cooked through; there should be no traces of pink when cutting through the thickest part of the meat.

4. Spread mayonnaise on the top half of each bun. Place a tomato slice and a lettuce leaf on the bottom half of each bun. Top with a chicken breast. Serve immediately with the coleslaw on the side.

PER SERVING: 965 CAL | FAT: 53.4 G | SAT FAT: 9 G | CARBS: 76.5 G | SUGARS: 19.8 G | FIBER: 8.3 G | PROTEIN: 41.8 G | SODIUM: 1,160 MG

BACON-WRAPPED CHICKEN BURGERS WITH GRILLED PINEAPPLE

THESE BURGERS ARE A REAL MIX OF GORGEOUS FLAVORS, WITH THE CHICKEN, BACON, PINEAPPLE, AND RUSSIAN DRESSING ALL PACKING A PUNCH.

PREP TIME: 20 MINUTES | COOK TIME: 25 MINUTES | SERVES: 4

8 smoked bacon strips

4 skinless, boneless chicken breasts

1 tablespoon vegetable oil, for brushing

1 Boston lettuce, shredded

4 brioche burger buns, halved

GRILLED PINEAPPLE

½ pineapple, peeled

1 tablespoon raw brown sugar

1 teaspoon pepper

RUSSIAN DRESSING

3 tablespoons mayonnaise

1 tablespoon ketchup

1 tablespoon horseradish

2 teaspoons hot pepper sauce

1 tablespoon Worcestershire sauce

1 shallot, grated

1. Lay two bacon strips next to each other on a cutting board. Place a chicken breast on top of the strips and wrap them all the way around the breast. Repeat with the remaining breasts.

2. To make the grilled pineapple, cut it into four thick rings, remove the core, then sprinkle each ring on both sides with sugar and pepper.

3. Preheat the barbecue grill to medium–high.

4. To make the dressing, mix the ingredients together in a bowl and set aside.

5. Brush the grate with oil, then place the chicken breasts on it. Cook for 10 minutes on each side, or until cooked through; there should be no traces of pink when cutting through the thickest part of the meat. Remove from the heat and let rest in a warm place for 4 minutes.

6. Meanwhile, grill the pineapple rings for 2 minutes on each side, or until caramelized.

7. Divide the lettuce among the burger buns and top each with a pineapple ring, chicken breast, and spoonful of dressing. Serve immediately.

PER SERVING: 641 CAL | FAT: 27.6 G | SAT FAT: 9.2 G | CARBS: 56 G | SUGARS: 17.3 G | FIBER: 4.8 G | PROTEIN: 40.9 G | SODIUM: 760 MG

TRADITIONAL CHICKEN BURGERS

NOTHING BEATS THE SIMPLICITY OF A TRADITIONAL BREADED CHICKEN BURGER.

PREP TIME: 25 MINUTES, PLUS CHILLING | COOK TIME: 14 MINUTES | SERVES: 4

4 large skinless, boneless chicken breasts

1 extra-large egg white

1 tablespoon cornstarch

1 tablespoon all-purpose flour

1 egg, beaten

1¼ cups fresh bread crumbs

2 tablespoons sunflower oil

4 burger buns, halved

4 Boston lettuce leaves

2 large tomatoes, sliced

¼ cup mayonnaise

1. Place each chicken breast between two sheets of plastic wrap and beat firmly with a meat mallet or rolling pin to flatten the chicken slightly. Beat together the egg white and cornstarch, then brush the mixture over the chicken. Cover and let chill for 30 minutes, then coat in the all-purpose flour.

2. Put the egg into a shallow dish and the bread crumbs in a separate shallow dish. Dip the chicken breasts first in the egg, letting any excess drip back into the dish, then in the bread crumbs, turning to coat.

3. Heat the oil in a heavy skillet over medium heat. Add the chicken and cook over medium heat for 6–8 minutes on each side, or until the chicken is tender and cooked through; there should be no traces of pink when cutting through the thickest part of the meat.

4. Serve the burgers in the burger buns with the lettuce, tomato slices, and mayonnaise.

PER SERVING: 558 CAL | FAT: 22.7 G | SAT FAT: 3.6 G | CARBS: 40.7 G | SUGARS: 5.2 G | FIBER: 4.1 G | PROTEIN: 44.1 G | SODIUM: 520 MG

JAPANESE-STYLE CHICKEN PATTIES

THESE FLAVORFUL BURGERS ARE BEST SERVED WITHOUT A BUN, ACCOMPANIED BY A TANGY MANGO SALSA INSTEAD.

PREP TIME: 15–20 MINUTES, PLUS CHILLING | COOK TIME: 10–15 MINUTES | SERVES: 4

1 pound fresh ground chicken

1 tablespoon grated fresh ginger

1 garlic clove, finely chopped

1 tablespoon ketjap manis
(Indonesian soy sauce)

½ bunch scallions, trimmed and
finely chopped

2 tablespoons vegetable oil

noodle salad (optional)

MANGO SALSA

1 large mango, peeled, pitted,
and diced

1 red onion, finely chopped

2 ripe tomatoes, finely chopped

1 fresh red jalapeño chile, seeded
and finely chopped

1 tablespoon chopped
fresh cilantro

2 tablespoons lime juice

½ teaspoon salt (optional)

1. Put the ground chicken, ginger, garlic, ketjap manis, and scallions into a bowl and use your fingertips to combine. Shape the mixture into four patties, transfer to a plate, cover, and let chill for at least 30 minutes.

2. To make the mango salsa, place the ingredients into a small bowl and season with salt, if using, and stir well.

3. Preheat a ridged grill pan over medium heat, then add the oil. Add the patties and cook for 5–6 minutes on each side, until the chicken is thoroughly cooked; there should be no traces of pink when cutting through the thickest part of the burger. Serve immediately with the mango salsa and a simple noodle salad, if using.

PER SERVING: 294 CAL | FAT: 10.8 G | SAT FAT: 1.6 G | CARBS: 24.5 G | SUGARS: 18.1 G | FIBER: 3.1 G | PROTEIN: 26.1 G | SODIUM: 160 MG

JAMAICAN JERK CHICKEN BURGERS

GROUND CHICKEN IS SPICED UP WITH JAMAICAN JERK SEASONING FOR THESE DELICIOUS BURGERS.

PREP TIME: 25 MINUTES | COOK TIME: 20 MINUTES | SERVES: 4

1 teaspoon packed light brown sugar

1 teaspoon ground ginger

½ teaspoon ground allspice

½ teaspoon dried thyme

½ teaspoon cayenne pepper

1 tablespoon lime juice

2 garlic cloves, finely chopped

1 pound fresh ground chicken

1 tablespoon vegetable oil

1 red bell pepper, seeded and cut into large flat pieces

1 teaspoon olive oil

1 teaspoon red wine vinegar

4 onion rolls, halved

4 Boston lettuce leaves

salt and pepper (optional)

1. Put the sugar, ginger, allspice, thyme, cayenne pepper, lime juice, garlic, and salt and pepper, if using, into a bowl and mix together. Add the chicken and gently mix to combine. Divide the mixture into four equal portions and shape each portion into a patty.

2. Put a ridged grill pan over medium–high heat and add the vegetable oil. Add the red bell pepper and cook for about 5 minutes, turning frequently, until blackened. Transfer to a bowl, cover with plastic wrap or a plate, and let steam for 5 minutes. Remove the skin and cut the flesh into strips. Toss with the olive oil and vinegar.

3. Put the patties into the pan and cook, covered, for about 5 minutes on each side, until brown and cooked through; there should be no traces of pink when cutting through the thickest part of the burger. Place the burgers in the rolls and top with the lettuce and red bell peppers. Serve immediately.

PER SERVING: 338 CAL | FAT: 9.8 G | SAT FAT: 1.4 G | CARBS: 30.3 G | SUGARS: 3.7 G | FIBER: 3.8 G | PROTEIN: 29.8 G | SODIUM: 40 MG

THAI PEANUT CHICKEN BURGERS

THESE JUICY THAI-SPICED BURGERS ARE TOPPED OFF WITH A SWEET-AND-SPICY PEANUT SAUCE.

PREP TIME: 30 MINUTES | COOK TIME: 10 MINUTES | SERVES: 4

1 tablespoon packed
light brown sugar

1 tablespoon soy sauce

1 tablespoon Thai fish sauce

1 tablespoon lemon grass

2 teaspoons curry powder

1 garlic clove, finely chopped

½ teaspoon cayenne pepper

1 pound fresh ground chicken

1 tablespoon peanut oil,
for brushing

4 French rolls, halved

4 pickled onions, thinly sliced

PEANUT SAUCE

⅓ cup chunky peanut butter

6 tablespoons coconut milk

2 tablespoons hot water,
plus extra if needed

1 tablespoon Thai fish sauce

1 tablespoon packed
light brown sugar

1 tablespoon soy sauce

2 teaspoons fresh lime juice

1 garlic clove, finely chopped

¼ teaspoon cayenne pepper

1. Put the sugar, soy sauce, fish sauce, lemon grass, curry powder, garlic, and cayenne pepper into a medium bowl, stir to combine, then mix in the chicken. Divide the meat into four equal portions, then use damp hands to shape each portion into a ½-inch-thick oval patty.

2. To make the peanut sauce, put all of the ingredients into a food processor or blender and process until smooth. Add more water to loosen, if necessary.

3. Lightly brush a ridged grill pan with the oil and put over medium–high heat. Add the patties and cook for 5 minutes, then turn and cook for an additional 5 minutes, until brown and cooked through; there should be no traces of pink when cutting through the thickest part of the burger.

4. Spread both halves of the rolls with the peanut sauce, then top with the burgers and some pickled onions. Serve immediately.

PER SERVING: 507 CAL | FAT: 25.9 G | SAT FAT: 8 G | CARBS: 35.5 G | SUGARS: 10.4 G | FIBER: 4.4 G | PROTEIN: 35.1 G | SODIUM: 1,680 MG

TRADITIONAL TURKEY BURGERS

LOW IN FAT BUT PACKED FULL OF FLAVOR, TURKEY BURGERS MAKE A DELIGHTFUL CHANGE
FROM THEIR BEEFY COUSINS AND WILL BE POPULAR WITH ALL THE FAMILY.

PREP TIME: 10 MINUTES | COOK TIME: 5 MINUTES | SERVES: 4

12 ounces fresh ground
turkey breast

¼ cup fresh whole-wheat
bread crumbs

1 small onion, finely chopped

1 apple, peeled, cored, and finely
chopped

grated zest and juice of
1 small lemon

2 tablespoons finely chopped
fresh parsley

sunflower oil, for brushing

4 multigrain rolls or focaccia, halved

salt and pepper (optional)

1. Preheat the broiler to medium—high and line the broiler pan with aluminum foil. Put the turkey, bread crumbs, onion, apple, lemon zest and juice, and parsley into a large bowl. Season with salt and pepper, if using, and gently mix to combine. Divide into four equal portions and shape each portion into a patty.

2. Brush the patties with oil and place under the preheated broiler. Cook, turning once, for 5 minutes, or until cooked through; there should be no traces of pink when cutting through the thickest part of the burger. If there are any traces of pink, return to the broiler for 1–2 minutes.

3. Place a burger on the bottom half of each bun, add the bun lids, and serve immediately.

PER SERVING: 331 CAL | FAT: 5.9 G | SAT FAT: 0.8 G | CARBS: 39.9 G | SUGARS: 7.7 G | FIBER: 4.5 G | PROTEIN: 28.6 G | SODIUM: 320 MG

TURKEY & TARRAGON BURGERS

TURKEY AND TARRAGON ADD DISTINCTIVE FLAVORS TO THESE BURGERS. SERVING ON A BED OF SALAD
INSTEAD OF A BUN MAKES THEM AN EXTRA-HEALTHY DINNER OPTION.

PREP TIME: 20 MINUTES, PLUS CHILLING | COOK TIME: 20–30 MINUTES | SERVES: 4

⅓ cup bulgur wheat

1 teaspoon salt, for cooking the
bulgur wheat

1 pound fresh ground turkey

1 tablespoon finely grated
orange zest

1 red onion, finely chopped

1 yellow bell pepper, peeled,
seeded, and finely chopped

¼ cup slivered almonds, toasted

1 tablespoon chopped fresh
tarragon

2 tablespoons sunflower oil,
for brushing

1 Boston lettuce, sliced

4 large tomatoes, quartered

1 red onion, finely sliced

salt and pepper (optional)

1. Bring a medium saucepan of lightly salted water to a boil, add the bulgur wheat, and
cook for 10–15 minutes, or according to the package directions.

2. Drain the bulgur wheat and place in a bowl with the ground turkey, orange zest, onion,
yellow bell pepper, almonds, tarragon, and salt and pepper, if using. Mix together, then
shape into four equal patties. Cover and let chill in the refrigerator for 1 hour.

3. Preheat the barbecue to medium–high. Brush the patties with the oil and cook for
5–6 minutes on each side, or until cooked through; there should be no traces of pink
when cutting through the thickest part of the burger.

4. Put some lettuce, tomato quarters, and onion slices onto four serving plates and place
a burger on top of each. Serve immediately.

PER SERVING: 336 CAL | FAT: 13.1 G | SAT FAT: 1.5 G | CARBS: 25.8 G | SUGARS: 7.6 G | FIBER: 6.9 G | PROTEIN: 31.4 G | SODIUM: 720 MG

MEXICAN TURKEY BURGERS

THESE SPICY TURKEY BURGERS ARE FILLED WITH GARLIC, JALAPEÑO CHILES, AND REFRIED BEANS, THEN TOPPED OFF WITH DOLLOPS OF SALSA AND FRESH GUACAMOLE.

PREP TIME: 25 MINUTES, PLUS CHILLING | COOK TIME: 10–12 MINUTES | SERVES: 4

1 pound fresh ground turkey

¾ cup canned refried beans

3 garlic cloves, crushed

1 fresh jalapeño chile, seeded and finely chopped

2 tablespoons tomato paste

1 tablespoon chopped fresh cilantro

2 tablespoons sunflower oil, for brushing

6 cups baby spinach leaves, shredded

4 cheese-topped burger buns, halved

salsa (optional)

tortilla chips, to serve (optional

salt and pepper (optional)

GUACAMOLE

1 tomato

2 limes

3 small ripe avocados, pitted and peeled

½ onion, finely chopped

¼ teaspoon ground cumin

¼ teaspoon mild chili powder

½ fresh green chile, such as jalapeño or serrano, seeded and finely chopped

1. To make the guacamole, put the tomato into a heatproof bowl, pour over boiling water to cover, and let stand for 30 seconds. Drain and plunge into cold water. Peel off the skin. Cut the tomato in half, seed, and chop the flesh.

2. Squeeze the juice from the limes into a small bowl. Dice the avocados and toss in the bowl of lime juice to prevent the flesh from discoloring. Coarsely mash the avocados with a fork.

3. Add the tomato, onion, cumin, chili powder, and chile to the avocados and mix together. Chill, covered, in the refrigerator until ready to serve.

4. Meanwhile, put the ground turkey into a bowl and break up any large lumps. Beat the refried beans until smooth, then add to the turkey in the bowl.

5. Add the garlic, chile, tomato paste, and cilantro with salt and pepper, if using, and mix together. Shape into four equal patties, then cover and chill in the refrigerator for 1 hour.

6. Preheat the barbecue grill to medium–high. Brush the patties with the oil and cook for 5–6 minutes on each side, or until cooked through; there should be no traces of pink when cutting through the thickest part of the burger.

7. Place the spinach on the bottom halves of the burger buns and top with the burgers. Spoon over a little salsa, if using, and guacamole and top with the lids. Serve immediately with tortilla chips on the side, if you want.

PER SERVING: 589 CAL | FAT: 26.4 G | SAT FAT: 6.4 G | CARBS: 49 G | SUGARS: 6.5 G | FIBER: 11 G | PROTEIN: 40.9 G | SODIUM: 720 MG

LEMON & MINT TURKEY BURGERS

THE COMBINATION OF LEMON AND MINT GIVES THESE BURGERS A LIGHT, REFRESHING FLAVOR.

PREP TIME: 10 MINUTES, PLUS CHILLING | COOK TIME: 15 MINUTES | MAKES: 12

1 pound 2 ounces fresh ground turkey

½ small onion, grated

finely grated zest and juice of 1 lemon

1 garlic clove, finely chopped

2 tablespoons finely chopped fresh mint

1 egg, beaten

1 tablespoon olive oil

salt and pepper (optional)

12 lemon wedges, to serve

1. Put the turkey, onion, lemon zest and juice, garlic, mint, egg, and salt and pepper, if using, into a bowl and mix well with a fork. Divide into 12 equal portions and shape each portion into a patty. Cover and chill in the refrigerator for at least 1 hour, or overnight.

2. Put the oil into a large, heavy skillet over medium–high heat. When hot, add the patties, cooking in batches, if necessary. Cook for 4–5 minutes on each side, until golden brown and cooked through; there should be no traces of pink when cutting through the thickest part of the burger.

3. Transfer the burgers to a warm serving plate and serve immediately with the lemon wedges for squeezing over the top.

PER SERVING: 69 CAL | FAT: 2.4 G | SAT FAT: 0.5 G | CARBS: 1.7 G | SUGARS: 0.6 G | FIBER: 0.2 G | PROTEIN: 10.1 G | SODIUM: 40 MG

SESAME TURKEY BURGERS WITH PONZU MAYO

PONZU SAUCE HAS ALL THE RIGHT FLAVORS ROLLED INTO ONE BOTTLE TO GARNISH THESE DELICIOUS, JUICY BURGERS.

PREP TIME: 20 MINUTES | COOK TIME: 10 MINUTES | SERVES: 4

1 pound fresh ground turkey

2 tablespoons sesame seeds

4 teaspoons soy sauce

1 teaspoon toasted sesame oil

1 teaspoon ground garlic

¼ cup mayonnaise

2 tablespoons ponzu sauce

4 burger buns, halved

1 cup lettuce

2 large tomatoes, sliced

½ teaspoon freshly ground black pepper

2 tablespoons soy sauce, to serve

1. Put the turkey into a medium bowl with the sesame seeds, soy sauce, oil, and garlic and gently mix to combine. Divide into four equal portions and shape each portion into a patty. Place the patties on a large baking sheet.

2. Preheat the broiler to high and place the rack below the heat. Place the patties on the rack and broil for 5 minutes, then turn and continue cooking for an additional 4–5 minutes, until cooked through; there should be no traces of pink when cutting through the thickest part of the burger.

3. Combine the mayonnaise and ponzu sauce in a small bowl (the mixture will be thin). Coat each cut side of the buns with the sauce, then add the burgers. Top with some lettuce and tomato slices, then sprinkle with pepper and a drizzle of soy sauce. Serve immediately.

PER SERVING: 429 CAL | FAT: 17.3 G | SAT FAT: 2.6 G | CARBS: 32.6 G | SUGARS: 5.5 G | FIBER: 3.7 G | PROTEIN: 34 G | SODIUM: 1,360 MG

TURKEY CLUB BURGERS

TAKING A CUE FROM CLUB SANDWICHES, WHICH STACK SLICED TURKEY WITH BACON, LETTUCE, AND TOMATO BETWEEN TOASTED BREAD, THESE BURGERS ARE LAYERED WITH FLAVOR.

PREP TIME: 20 MINUTES | COOK TIME: 20 MINUTES | SERVES: 4

1 pound fresh ground turkey

1 garlic clove, finely chopped

½ teaspoon fresh rosemary

6 bacon strips

8 sourdough or country-style bread slices, toasted

3 tablespoons ranch-style dressing

4 Boston lettuce leaves

2 large tomatoes, sliced

salt and pepper (optional)

1. Preheat the barbecue to medium–high. Combine the ground turkey with the garlic, rosemary, and salt and pepper, if using, in a bowl. Divide the mixture into four equal portions and shape each portion into a thick patty.

2. Cook the bacon in a skillet over medium heat for about 8 minutes, or until crisp. Drain on paper towels and break the pieces in half.

3. Spread each slice of toasted bread with half of the ranch-style dressing.

4. Put the patties onto the rack and cook over medium heat, covered, for 4–5 minutes on each side, or until cooked through; there should be no traces of pink when cutting through the thickest part of the burger.

5. Place each burger on a slice of bread, add the bacon, lettuce, and tomato slices, drizzle with a little more dressing and top with the remaining toasted bread. Serve immediately.

PER SERVING: 493 CAL | FAT: 14.4 G | SAT FAT: 3.9 G | CARBS: 55.1 G | SUGARS: 10.2 G | FIBER: 2.7 G | PROTEIN: 34.9 G | SODIUM: 1,240 MG

TURKEY & BLUE CHEESE BURGERS

LEAVE BLAND TURKEY BURGERS BEHIND WITH THESE DELICIOUS ONES FILLED WITH BLUE CHEESE AND BLACK PEPPER.

PREP TIME: 10 MINUTES | COOK TIME: 10 MINUTES | SERVES: 4

2 shallots, finely chopped

½ teaspoon salt

½ teaspoon pepper

½ cup crumbled Gorgonzola cheese or other blue cheese

1 pound fresh ground turkey

4 crusty bread rolls, halved

1. Preheat the barbecue grill to medium–high. Put the shallots, salt, pepper, and cheese into a bowl and combine. Add the turkey and gently break up the meat while working all the ingredients together.

2. Divide the mixture into four equal portions and shape each portion into a patty.

3. Place the patties on the grate and cook for about 4 minutes on each side, until brown and cooked through; there should be no traces of pink when cutting through the thickest part of the burger. Place the burgers in the buns and serve immediately.

PER SERVING: 399 CAL | FAT: 6.9 G | SAT FAT: 3.6 G | CARBS: 46.9 G | SUGARS: 3.3 G | FIBER: 2.4 G | PROTEIN: 35.1 G | SODIUM: 920 MG

CHAPTER THREE

VEGGIE & VEGAN

AVOCADO BURGERS WITH QUINOA PATTIES

BURGERS DON'T NEED TO BE UNHEALTHY. HEALTH-BOOSTING AVOCADO ENCASES WELL-SEASONED QUINOA FOR A QUICK AND TASTY SUPERFOOD OPTION.

PREP TIME: 20 MINUTES, PLUS CHILLING | COOK TIME: 25 MINUTES | SERVES: 4

1¼ cups quinoa

1 small onion

1 garlic clove

½ cup drained sun-dried tomatoes in oil

1 egg, beaten

4 avocados

2 tablespoons olive oil, for frying

¼ cup cream cheese

½ green bell pepper, seeded and sliced into rings

1 tablespoon poppy seeds

salt and pepper (optional)

1. For the patties, cook the quinoa according to the package directions and let cool.

2. Put the onion, garlic, and sun-dried tomatoes into a food processor and pulse until minced. Alternatively, finely chop them by hand. Put this mixture into a large mixing bowl, along with the quinoa and egg, and season with salt and pepper, if using. Using your hands, mix everything together and shape the mixture into four patties about the size of your palm and 1 inch thick. Put onto a plate and chill in the refrigerator for 30 minutes, until firm.

3. Meanwhile, prepare the avocado. Cut the avocado in half around the middle and remove the pit. For the top half of the avocado, being as gentle as possible, make a cut in the top, and peel away the skin to reveal the flesh. Repeat for the bottom half, and then slice off the base so it can stand.

4. Heat the olive oil in a shallow nonstick skillet and sauté the patties for about 2 minutes on each side, until they are golden and crisp.

5. Fill the center of the avocado with a quinoa patty, cream cheese, and a ring of green pepper. Sprinkle poppy seeds over the top and serve.

PER SERVING: 563 CAL | FAT: 34.9 G | SAT FAT: 7 G | CARBS: 54.4 G | SUGARS: 7.5 G | FIBER: 14.5 G | PROTEIN: 14.5 G | SODIUM: 80 MG

TRADITIONAL VEGGIE BURGERS

A FANTASTIC BURGER FOR VEGETARIANS AND NONVEGETARIANS ALIKE, FULL OF FLAVOR, TEXTURE, AND HEALTHY INGREDIENTS.

PREP TIME: 10 MINUTES, PLUS CHILLING | COOK TIME: 35 MINUTES | SERVES: 4

½ cup brown rice

1½ cups drained and rinsed, canned great Northern beans

1 cup unsalted cashew nuts

3 garlic cloves

1 red onion, cut into wedges

¾ cup corn kernels

2 tablespoons tomato paste

1 tablespoon chopped fresh oregano

2 tablespoons whole-wheat flour

2 tablespoons sunflower oil

1 Boston lettuce, shredded

4 whole-wheat buns, halved

2 large tomatoes, sliced

4 vegetarian halloumi cheese slices

salt and pepper (optional)

1. Cook the rice in a saucepan of boiling water for 20 minutes, or according to package directions, until tender. Drain and put into a food processor or blender.

2. Add the beans, cashew nuts, garlic, onion, corn, tomato paste, oregano, and salt and pepper, if using, to the rice in the food processor and, using the pulse button, blend together. Shape into four equal patties, then coat in the flour. Cover and let chill in the refrigerator for 1 hour.

3. Preheat the barbecue grill to medium–high. Brush the patties with the oil and cook for 5–6 minutes on each side, or until cooked through.

4. Place the shredded lettuce leaves on the bottom halves of the buns and top with the burgers. Top each with tomato slices and a halloumi cheese slice. Place under a hot broiler for 2 minutes, or until golden brown. Add the bun lids and serve immediately.

PER SERVING: 672 CAL | FAT: 31.5 G | SAT FAT: 9.3 G | CARBS: 74.4 G | SUGARS: 12.2 G | FIBER: 12.1 G | PROTEIN: 26.8 G | SODIUM: 560 MG

VEGAN BBQ JACKFRUIT BURGER

IT WOULD BE HARD TO TELL FROM FIRST GLANCE THAT THIS ISN'T PULLED PORK. JACKFRUIT BREAKS EASILY INTO SHREDS WITH TWO FORKS, AND WITH HOMEMADE BARBECUE SAUCE IT HAS ALL THE FLAVOR BUT LESS FAT.

PREP TIME: 15 MINUTES | COOK TIME: 15–17 MINUTES | SERVES: 4

1⅔ cups canned jackfruit, drained

4 vegan whole-wheat seeded rolls, halved

1 small Boston lettuce, leaves separated and torn into pieces

BARBECUE SAUCE

1 tablespoon sunflower oil

1 onion, finely chopped

1 crisp apple, cored but not peeled, diced

2 tablespoons molasses sugar

2 tablespoons apple cider vinegar

1 tablespoon tomato paste

1 teaspoon dried oregano

2 teaspoons Dijon mustard

¼ teaspoon chili powder

¼ teaspoon ground allspice (optional)

COLESLAW

1¾ cups cups finely shredded red cabbage

¾ cup shredded carrot

juice of ½ unwaxed lemon

2 tablespoons freshly chopped cilantro or parsley

1. Put the drained jackfruit onto a cutting board and cut away the woody core in the center, then pull the fruit into thin shreds with two forks.

2. To make the barbecue sauce, heat the oil in a medium saucepan, then add the onion and apple, cover, and cook over low heat for 10 minutes, stirring from time to time until the onion and apple have softened. Add the molasses, vinegar, tomato paste, oregano, mustard, and chili powder, then the allspice, if using. Mix together and cook for 2–3 minutes, stirring.

3. Add the jackfruit to the barbecue sauce and cook for 3–4 minutes, stirring from time to time, until piping-hot and mixed thoroughly with the sauce.

4. To make the coleslaw, add the cabbage, carrot, and lemon juice to a bowl and fork together. Sprinkle the chopped cilantro or parsley over the top and mix together lightly.

5. Toast each side of the rolls until lightly browned. Transfer to serving plates. Cover the bottom half of each roll with the torn lettuce leaves. Reheat the jackfruit, if needed, then spoon onto the rolls. Add a spoonful of coleslaw to each and cover with the roll tops. Serve immediately.

PER SERVING: 418 CAL | FAT: 12.1 G | SAT FAT: 0.7 G | CARBS: 67.1 G | SUGARS: 31.7 G | FIBER: 10.7 G | PROTEIN: 12.1 G | SODIUM: 280 MG

CLOUD BREAD BREAKFAST BURGER

CLOUD BREAD IS A FANTASTIC OPTION IF YOU WANT A LOW-CARB MEAL. THESE BURGERS FILLED WITH GUACAMOLE AND CHEESE MAKE A HEARTY BREAKFAST DISH, BUT THEY CAN BE SERVED UP ANY TIME OF DAY.

 PREP TIME: 15 MINUTES | COOK TIME: 25 MINUTES | SERVES: 4

2 teaspoons extra virgin canola oil

1 large tomato, thickly sliced into four rounds

3½ ounces buffalo mozzarella cheese, drained and sliced into four rounds

CLOUD BREAD BUNS

8 sprays cooking oil spray

3 extra-large eggs, separated

¾ teaspoon baking powder

⅓ cup Greek-style yogurt

1½ tablespoons cream cheese

¼ teaspoon pureed garlic or prepared garlic paste

¼ teaspoon salt

3 tablespoons plain whey protein powder

GUACAMOLE

1 large ripe avocado, peeled and pitted

½ medium-hot red chile, seeded and finely chopped

½ small red onion, chopped

juice of ½ lime

⅓ cup chopped fresh cilantro

salt and pepper (optional)

1. First make the buns. Preheat the oven to 300°F. Line two baking sheets with baking parchment and lightly spray with the cooking oil.

2. Put the egg whites into a mixing bowl with the baking powder and whisk with a handheld electric mixer until they hold stiff peaks. Set aside.

3. Combine the egg yolks in a bowl with the remaining bun ingredients, stirring well. Fold the egg whites into the yolk mixture a little at a time—don't overmix.

4. Using a large spoon, place eight mounds of the egg mixture on the prepared sheets, each about the diameter of a burger bun. Bake in the middle of the preheated oven for 20 minutes, or until the buns are light golden and puffed up. Transfer to wire racks and let cool (they will sink a little).

5. To make the guacamole, put the avocado into a bowl with the chile, red onion, lime juice, cilantro leaves, and salt and pepper to taste, if using. Mash with a fork, leaving a few small chunks of avocado for texture.

6. To assemble the burgers, spread the flat sides of the cloud buns with the oil and lightly toast under the broiler.

7. Spread the guacamole on the toasted sides of four of the buns, then add a layer of sliced tomato and top with the cheese rounds. Return them to the broiler for a few minutes to melt the cheese, then place the remaining four buns on top to serve.

PER SERVING: 323 CAL | FAT: 24.3 G | SAT FAT: 8.5 G | CARBS: 9.6 G | SUGARS: 3.1 G | FIBER: 4 G | PROTEIN: 18.9 G | SODIUM: 400 MG

QUINOA & BEET BURGERS

HERE'S A BURGER WITH A DIFFERENCE. IT WILL BRING A SHADE OF PURPLE TO YOUR PLATE, BUT IN TRUE BURGER TRADITION, IT STILL PROVIDES A TASTY TREAT.

PREP TIME: 35 MINUTES | 1 HOUR 10 MINUTES | SERVES: 8

3–4 small beets (about 8 ounces), peeled and cubed

¾ cup quinoa, rinsed

1½ cups vegetable broth

½ small onion, grated

finely grated zest of ½ lemon

2 teaspoons cumin seeds

½ teaspoon salt

¼ teaspoon pepper

1 extra-large egg white, lightly beaten

¾ cup quinoa flour, for dusting

1 tablespoon vegetable oil, for pan-frying

8 slices of sourdough toast, to serve

5½ cups peppery salad greens, to serve

WASABI BUTTER

1½ teaspoons wasabi powder

¾ teaspoon warm water

5 tablespoons butter, at room temperature

1. Cook the beets in a steamer for 1 hour.

2. Meanwhile, put the quinoa into a saucepan with the broth. Bring to a boil, then cover and simmer over low heat for 10 minutes. Remove from the heat, but keep the pan covered for an additional 10 minutes to let the grains swell. Fluff up with a fork and spread out on a baking sheet to dry.

3. To make the wasabi butter, mix together the wasabi powder and water. Mix with the butter and chill in the refrigerator.

4. Put the beets into a food processor and process until smooth. Transfer to a bowl and mix with the quinoa, onion, lemon zest, cumin seeds, salt, pepper, and egg white.

5. Divide the mixture into eight equal portions and shape into patties, each ⅝ inch thick, firmly pressing the mixture together. Lightly dust with quinoa flour.

6. Heat a thin layer of oil in a nonstick skillet. Add the patties and cook over medium-high heat, in batches if necessary, for 2 minutes on each side, turning carefully.

7. Place the burgers on the toast and serve with the wasabi butter and salad greens.

PER SERVING: 281 CAL | FAT: 11 G | SAT FAT: 5 G | CARBS: 35 G | SUGARS: 5 G | FIBER: 4 G | PROTEIN: 9 G | SODIUM 520 MG

VEGAN SPINACH & LENTIL BURGERS WITH SWEET POTATO BUN

A TASTY BURGER AND BUN RECIPE THAT EVERYONE—NOT JUST VEGANS—WILL ENJOY. SPIRALIZED SWEET POTATO MAKES AN IDEAL LOW-CARB REPLACEMENT FOR BREAD.

PREP TIME: 12 MINUTES, PLUS CHILLING AND SOAKING | COOK TIME: 25 MINUTES | SERVES: 2

BUNS

1 large sweet potato (about 9 ounces)

1 tablespoon extra virgin olive oil, plus 2 teaspoons for brushing

1½ teaspoons ground chia seeds

1½ tablespoons water

salt and pepper (optional)

BURGERS

1 tablespoon olive oil

½ small onion, finely chopped

1 garlic clove, crushed

¾ cup finely chopped cremini mushrooms

1½ teaspoons ground chia seeds

1½ tablespoons water

2¼ cups washed spinach

½ cup cooked brown lentils

1 teaspoon crushed red pepper flakes

4 lettuce leaves

salt and pepper (optional)

1. To make the buns, cut the pointed ends off the sweet potato. Spiralize the potato. Add two-thirds of the oil to a skillet, then add the sweet potato and sauté over medium heat for 4–5 minutes, until soft. Let cool. Meanwhile, put the chia seeds into a small bowl with the water and set aside for 15 minutes.

2. Combine the sweet potato, chia seeds, and salt and pepper, if using, in a bowl so that each strand has a coating of the chia mix. Brush four 1-cup ramekins with oil, then divide the sweet potato mixture among them. Press down until the ramekins are about ¾-inch deep with the mix, cover with plastic wrap, and put a filled jar on top of each ramekin. Let stand for 30 minutes.

3. To make the patties, heat half the oil in a small nonstick skillet, then add the onion and garlic and sauté over medium heat, stirring frequently, for 3 minutes, until soft. Add the mushrooms and stir for an additional 2 minutes. Set aside.

4. Put the chia seeds into a small bowl with the water and set aside for 15 minutes. Cook the spinach for 2 minutes or until just cooked. Squeeze out as much liquid as you can, then chop.

5. Put the lentils into a food processor and pulse for a few seconds, or mash using a pestle and mortar. Transfer to a mixing bowl, add the mushroom mix, spinach, chia seeds, red pepper flakes, and salt and pepper, if using. Shape into two patties.

6. Heat the remaining oil in a nonstick skillet over medium heat, then carefully add the patties and cook for about 3 minutes on each side, until golden and firm.

7. Meanwhile, heat the remaining oil from the bun recipe in a separate skillet, add the sweet potato buns, and cook over medium-high heat for 3 minutes on each side or until golden.

8. Serve the burgers inside the sweet potato buns with the lettuce leaves.

PER SERVING: 384 CAL | FAT: 20.6 G | SAT FAT: 2.6 G | CARBS: 43.5 G | SUGARS: 8 G | FIBER: 11.8 G | PROTEIN: 9.3 G | SODIUM: 80 MG

BEAN BURGERS

RED KIDNEY BEANS AND CHICKPEAS FILL OUT THESE HEARTY VEGETARIAN BURGERS.

PREP TIME: 15 MINUTES | COOK TIME: 10–12 MINUTES | SERVES: 4

1⅔ cups drained and rinsed, canned red kidney beans

1½ cups drained and rinsed, canned chickpeas

1 egg yolk

¼ teaspoon smoked paprika

1 cup fresh bread crumbs

3 scallions, finely chopped

2 tablespoons sunflower oil, for brushing

4 crusty bread rolls, halved

4 Boston lettuce leaves

2 large tomatoes, sliced

¼ cup sour cream

salt and pepper (optional)

1. Preheat the barbecue grill to high.

2. Put the beans, chickpeas, egg yolk, paprika, bread crumbs, and scallions into a large bowl and gently mix to combine. Season with salt and pepper, if using.

3. Divide the mixture into four equal portions and shape each portion into a patty. Season the outside of the patties with salt and pepper, if using, and lightly brush with oil.

4. Oil the barbecue grate. Cook the patties for 5 minutes on each side, or until cooked through. Brush the inside of the buns with oil and toast over the grill, cut side down, for 1–2 minutes.

5. Place the lettuce and tomatoes on bottom half of each bun, then top with the burgers and sour cream. Add the bun lids and serve immediately.

PER SERVING: 496 CAL | FAT: 12.9 G | SAT FAT: 2.6 G | CARBS: 72 G | SUGARS: 6.3 G | FIBER: 12 G | PROTEIN: 18.6 G | SODIUM: 360 MG

VEGAN KALE & BLACK BEAN SLOPPY JOE

BEING VEGAN DOESN'T MEAN MISSING OUT. THIS MEATLESS VERSION OF A TRADITIONAL TREAT IS JUST AS DELICIOUS AND FILLING AS THE ORIGINAL.

PREP TIME: 15 MINUTES | COOK TIME: 40 MINUTES | SERVES: 4

2 sweet potatoes, cut into 8 wedges

¼ cup olive oil

½ teaspoon salt

½ teaspoon pepper

2 avocados, peeled, pitted, and sliced

4 vegan burger buns, halved

SLOPPY JOE

2 tablespoons olive oil

2 garlic cloves, crushed

¼ teaspoon crushed red pepper flakes

1 teaspoon cumin powder

1 teaspoon coriander powder

1 teaspoon mild paprika

½ teaspoon dried oregano

1 tablespoon packed light brown sugar

⅔ cup canned diced tomatoes

⅔ cup cored and shredded kale

½ cup drained and rinsed, canned black beans

salt and pepper (optional)

1. Preheat the oven to 350°F.

2. Put the potatoes into a bowl and add the oil, salt, and pepper. Toss well to coat. Arrange the potatoes in a single layer on a nonstick baking pan and bake in the oven for 25–30 minutes, until golden brown and tender.

3. Meanwhile, to make the sloppy joe, heat the oil in a medium saucepan over low heat and add the garlic and crushed red pepper flakes. Gently cook until the garlic starts to turn golden. Add the spices and salt and pepper, if using. Stir for a few seconds, then add the sugar, diced tomatoes, and kale. Cook for 5 minutes, or until the kale has wilted. Add the black beans and cook for an additional minute.

4. Toast the burger buns and place two slices of avocado and two potato wedges on the bottom half of each bun. Spoon the kale and black bean sloppy joe on top.

5. Add the bun lids and serve immediately.

PER SERVING: 550 CAL | FAT: 33.1 G | SAT FAT: 4.7 G | CARBS: 54.4 G | SUGARS: 11 G | FIBER: 10.7 G | PROTEIN: 10.6 G | SODIUM: 560 MG

SWEET POTATO & HALLOUMI BURGERS

THERE ARE SO MANY INTERESTING TEXTURES AND FLAVORS VYING FOR YOUR ATTENTION IN THESE TASTY VEGETARIAN BURGERS THAT A BUN ISN'T REQUIRED.

PREP TIME: 20 MINS, PLUS CHILLING | COOK TIME: 40–50 MINUTES | SERVES: 4

2–3 sweet potatoes (about 1 pound), cut into chunks

2½ cups small broccoli floret pieces

2 garlic cloves, crushed

1 red onion, finely chopped or grated

1½ fresh red jalapeño chiles, seeded and finely chopped

6 ounces vegetarian halloumi cheese, grated

2 tablespoons whole-wheat flour

2 tablespoons sunflower oil

4 onions (about 1 pound), sliced

1 tablespoon chopped fresh cilantro

salt and pepper (optional)

1. Add a little salt, if using, to a saucepan of water and bring to a boil. Add the sweet potato and cook for 15–20 minutes, or until tender. Drain and mash. Bring a separate saucepan of water to a boil, add the broccoli, and cook for 3 minutes, then drain and plunge into cold water. Drain again, then add to the mashed sweet potatoes.

2. Stir in the garlic, red onion, chiles, halloumi cheese, and salt and pepper, if using. Mix well and shape into four equal patties, then coat in the flour. Cover and chill in the refrigerator for at least 1 hour.

3. Heat 1½ tablespoons of the oil in a heavy skillet. Add the onions and sauté over medium heat for 12–15 minutes, or until soft. Stir in the cilantro and set aside.

4. Place the patties in the pan, adding more oil if necessary. Cook over medium heat for 5–6 minutes on each side, or until they are cooked through.

5. Top the burgers with the fried onions and cilantro and serve.

PER SERVING: 396 CAL | FAT: 18.7 G | SAT FAT: 8.7 G | CARBS: 44.1 G | SUGARS: 12.9 G | FIBER: 7.6 G | PROTEIN: 15.6 G | SODIUM: 520 MG

VEGAN TOFU BURGERS WITH CILANTRO-GARLIC MAYONNAISE

TOFU IS AN EXCELLENT SOURCE OF PROTEIN AND IS IDEAL FOR VEGETARIANS, VEGANS, AND MEAT-EATERS ALIKE.

PREP TIME: 15 MINUTES, PLUS MARINATING | COOK TIME: 6 MINUTES | SERVES: 3

10 ounces firm tofu

2 tablespoons soy sauce

½ teaspoon vegan Worcestershire sauce

1 garlic clove, finely chopped

¼ teaspoon crushed red pepper flakes

8 small fresh cilantro sprigs, coarsely chopped

¼ cup vegan mayonnaise

3 vegan burger buns, halved

½ small red onion, thinly sliced

3 Boston lettuce leaves

1. Preheat the broiler to high and place the rack about 6 inches below the heat. Line the broiler pan with aluminum foil.

2. Drain the tofu and pat dry. Slice into ½-inch-thick slabs that will fit in the buns and drain on paper towels.

3. Combine the soy sauce, Worcestershire sauce, half the garlic, and the red pepper flakes in a shallow dish wide enough to fit the tofu in a single layer. Place the tofu in the mixture, then turn to coat on both sides. Place in the refrigerator and marinate for at least 15 minutes or for up to 3 hours.

4. Put the cilantro and the remaining garlic into a small food processor or blender and puree. Add the mayonnaise and mix until smooth.

5. Transfer the tofu to the prepared pan. Cook under the preheated broiler for 3 minutes on each side, or until brown.

6. Spread the cilantro-garlic mayonnaise on both halves of the buns, then add one-third of the tofu to bottom half of each bun. Add the onion and lettuce, finish with the top halves of the buns, and serve immediately.

PER SERVING: 321 CAL | FAT: 14.8 G | SAT FAT: 2.2 G | CARBS: 33.4 G | SUGARS: 4.9 G | FIBER: 3.2 G | PROTEIN: 15.2 G | SODIUM: 880 MG

PORTOBELLO MUSHROOM BURGERS WITH MOZZARELLA

THIS VEGETARIAN BURGER COMBINES MARINATED PORTOBELLO MUSHROOMS WITH MOZZARELLA CHEESE AND PESTO IN A FOCACCIA "BUN."

PREP TIME: 10 MINUTES | COOK TIME: 15 MINUTES | SERVES: 4

4 teaspoons olive oil

2 teaspoons red wine vinegar

1 garlic clove, finely chopped

4 large Portobello mushrooms, caps only

8 slices fresh vegetarian mozzarella-style cheese

4 (6-inch-square) pieces focaccia, halved

¼ cup vegetarian basil pesto

2 large tomatoes, sliced

baby arugula leaves (optional)

salt and pepper (optional)

1. Preheat the broiler to high and the oven to 325°F. Whisk together the oil, vinegar, and garlic in a medium bowl. Place the mushrooms gill side up on a baking pan, then drizzle with the vinaigrette and season with salt and pepper, if using.

2. Place under the preheated broiler and cook for about 5–8 minutes, until the mushrooms are tender. Place the cheese slices on top and cook for an additional 1–2 minutes, until bubbling. Meanwhile, put the focaccia on a lower rack in the preheated oven for 5 minutes to warm through.

3. Lightly spread the focaccia with the pesto, then add the mushrooms. Top with the tomato slices and arugula, if using. Serve immediately.

PER SERVING: 501 CAL | FAT: 27.7 G | SAT FAT: 8.3 G | CARBS: 41 G | SUGARS: 4.7 G | FIBER: 3.6 G | PROTEIN: 22.6 G | SODIUM: 960 MG

VEGAN BENTO BURGERS

THESE JAPANESE VEGAN SNACKS ARE MADE WITH COOKED RICE PRESSED INTO THE SHAPE OF BUNS, CRISP ON THE OUTSIDE, WITH SAVORY SPINACH INSIDE.

PREP TIME: 15 MINUTES, PLUS RESTING | COOK TIME: 15 MINUTES | SERVES: 5

8 shiitake mushrooms, stems removed

1 pound spinach leaves, washed

2 tablespoons soy sauce

2 tablespoons mirin

2 teaspoons sesame seeds, toasted

1 teaspoon salt

1 cup lukewarm water

2½ cups short- or medium-grain white rice, rinsed, cooked, and kept warm

2 teaspoons sesame oil, for frying

1. Preheat the broiler to high. Arrange the mushrooms on the broiler pan and cook for 3 minutes on each side, until brown and tender. Thinly slice the mushrooms and put into a medium bowl.

2. Bring a large saucepan of water to a boil. Add the spinach and blanch for 1 minute. Drain, cool under cold running water, then squeeze dry. Add the mushrooms to the spinach, then add the soy sauce, mirin, and sesame seeds and combine.

3. Dissolve the salt in the warm water. Place the rice in a wide bowl and divide into ten equal portions. Wet your hands with the water and firmly press each portion into a rice bun. Wet your hands each time you make a bun. Let set for 20 minutes.

4. Place a nonstick skillet or ridged grill pan over medium heat and lightly coat the bottom with oil. Add the buns and cook for 4 minutes on each side (turning gently), until brown.

5. Put the spinach mixture on top of half the rice buns, then top with the remaining buns. Wrap the burgers in squares of parchment paper to hold them together prior to serving and serve within 2 hours.

PER SERVING: 375 CAL | FAT: 3.4 G | SAT FAT: 0.5 G | CARBS: 74.8 G | SUGARS: 2.9 G | FIBER: 3.6 G | PROTEIN: 9.4 G | SODIUM: 920 MG

VEGGIE BURGER BOWL

THESE BURGERS ARE FILLING AND NUTRITIOUS AND YOU COULD EAT THEM IN A BUN, BUT SERVING THEM IN A BOWL ON A BED OF COLORFUL ROASTED RATATOUILLE IS EVEN BETTER.

PREP TIME: 25 MINUTES, PLUS 20 MINUTES CHILLING | COOK TIME: 35–40 MINUTES | SERVES: 4

2 red bell peppers, seeded and chopped

2 yellow bell peppers, seeded and chopped

2 red onions, cut into wedges

2 zucchini, thickly sliced

3 tablespoons olive oil

1½ cups drained and rinsed, canned chickpeas

1⅓ cups frozen peas, thawed

1⅓ cups frozen corn, thawed

4 sprigs fresh cilantro

¼ teaspoon ground cumin

⅔ cup all-purpose flour

1 tablespoon sunflower seeds

1 tablespoon sesame seeds

salt and pepper (optional)

DRESSING

1 avocado, peeled, pitted, and chopped

¾ cup plain yogurt

2 scallions, chopped

1 garlic clove, crushed

1 tablespoon lime juice

salt and pepper (optional)

1. Preheat the oven to 400°F.

2. Put the red bell peppers, yellow bell peppers, onions, and zucchini into a roasting pan and drizzle with 1 tablespoon of the oil. Roast for 35–40 minutes, until they are slightly charred at the edges.

3. Meanwhile, put the chickpeas, peas, corn, cilantro, cumin, and ½ cup of the flour into a food processor and process to a thick paste. Add the sunflower seeds and sesame seeds, season with salt and pepper, if using, and process again to mix together.

4. Using wet hands, divide the mixture into four portions and shape each portion into a patty. Dust the patties with the remaining flour and chill in the refrigerator for 20 minutes.

5. Meanwhile, to make the dressing, put the avocado, yogurt, scallions, garlic, and lime juice into a small blender and blend until smooth. Season with salt and pepper, if using.

6. Heat the remaining oil in a skillet, add the patties, and cook for 5–6 minutes on each side, until cooked through.

7. Divide the roasted ratatouille among four bowls, top each portion with a burger, then drizzle with the dressing and serve immediately.

PER SERVING: 534 CAL | FAT: 24 G | SAT FAT: 4 G | CARBS: 66 G | SUGARS: 18.6 G | FIBER: 15.8 G | PROTEIN: 16.9 G | SODIUM: 40 MG

BEET, ZUCCHINI & CARROT BURGERS

THE TANGY YOGURT SAUCE CONTRASTS WITH THE SWEET, EARTHY VEGETABLES IN THESE THESE WHOLESOME, CRISP BURGERS.

PREP TIME: 30 MINUTES, PLUS STANDING AND CHILLING | COOK TIME: 35–40 MINUTES | SERVES: 5

½ cup millet

¾ cup lightly salted water

2 raw beets, grated

¼ cup shredded carrots

1½ cups shredded zucchini

½ cup finely chopped walnuts

2 tablespoons apple cider vinegar

2 tablespoons extra virgin olive oil, plus extra for frying

1 egg, beaten

2 tablespoons cornstarch

5 multigrain buns, halved

5 Boston lettuce leaves

salt and pepper (optional)

YOGURT SAUCE

1 cup plain yogurt

2 teaspoons finely chopped garlic

salt and pepper (optional)

1. Rinse and drain the millet and put it into a small saucepan with the salted water. Put over medium heat, bring to a simmer, cover, and cook over low heat for 20–25 minutes, or according to the package directions, until tender. Remove from the heat and let stand for 5 minutes, covered.

2. Put the beets, carrots, zucchini, and walnuts into a large bowl. Add the millet, vinegar, oil, salt and pepper, if using, and mix well. Add the egg and cornstarch, mix again, then chill in the refrigerator for 2 hours.

3. To make the sauce, put the yogurt in a fine strainer over a bowl and drain for at least 30 minutes. Stir in the garlic and season with salt and pepper, if using.

4. Pack the beet mixture into a ½ cup-capacity measuring cup, then shape into a patty. Repeat to make a total of five patties. Put a ridged grill pan or large skillet over medium heat and coat with oil. Add the patties and cook for about 5 minutes on each side, turning carefully, until brown.

5. Spread the buns with the yogurt sauce and place the burgers in the buns, topped with the lettuce. Serve immediately.

PER SERVING: 471 CAL | FAT: 20.5 G | SAT FAT: 3.5 G | CARBS: 59.3 G | SUGARS: 8.8 G | FIBER: 6.2 G | PROTEIN: 15 G | SODIUM: 360 MG

VEGAN BUTTERNUT SQUASH & POLENTA BURGERS

POLENTA, AN ITALIAN VERSION OF CORNMEAL, IS A FANTASTIC ADDITION TO THESE VEGAN BURGERS.

PREP TIME: 20 MINUTES, PLUS CHILLING | COOK TIME: 40 MINUTES | SERVES: 4

½ butternut squash (about 1 pound), peeled, seeded, and chopped

⅔ cup water

½ cup instant polenta or coarse cornmeal

1⅓ cups peeled and shredded celeriac

6 scallions, finely chopped

1 cup chopped pecans

2 tablespoons chopped fresh mixed herbs

2 tablespoons whole-wheat flour

1 tablespoon sunflower oil, for oiling

4 vegan burger buns, halved and toasted

2 large tomatoes, sliced

watercress or other peppery greens (optional)

salt and pepper (optional)

1. Bring a large saucepan of water to a boil, add the butternut squash, bring back to a boil, and cook for 15–20 minutes, or until tender. Drain and finely chop or mash. Put the measured water into a separate saucepan and bring to a boil. Slowly pour in the polenta or cornmeal in a steady stream and cook over low heat, stirring constantly, for 5 minutes, or according to the package directions, until thick.

2. Remove the pan from the heat and stir in the squash, celeriac, scallions, nuts, herbs, and salt and pepper, if using. Mix well, then shape into four equal patties. Coat the patties in the flour, cover, and chill in the refrigerator for 1 hour. Meanwhile, preheat the barbecue grill to medium–high.

3. Oil the grate. Lightly brush the patties with oil and cook for 5–6 minutes on each side, or until cooked through. Transfer to serving plates and serve immediately in the burger buns topped with tomato slices and watercress or other peppery greens, if using.

PER SERVING: 558 CAL | FAT: 28.1 G | SAT FAT: 2.8 G | CARBS: 69.4 G | SUGARS: 8.4 G | FIBER: 9.6 G | PROTEIN: 12.5 G | SODIUM: 240 MG

GREENS, PEAS & BEANS BURGERS

A MIXTURE OF PEPPERY GREENS ADDS COLOR AND NUTRIENTS TO THESE MOUTHWATERING VEGGIE BURGERS. THEY ARE LIGHT YET FULL OF FLAVOR—EVEN MEAT-EATERS WILL DEVOUR THEM.

PREP TIME: 30 MINUTES, PLUS STANDING | COOK TIME: 10 MINUTES | SERVES: 8

4 cups peppery greens, such as arugula, mustard greens, bok choy (green part only), or a mixture, thick stems removed

⅓ cup cooked peas, mashed

1½ cups drained and rinsed, canned lima beans, mashed

1 tablespoon grated onion

1½ tablespoons chopped fresh mint

1 egg, beaten

⅓ cup dry bread crumbs

3 tablespoons vegetable oil

4 whole-wheat pita breads, halved widthwise

16 cherry tomatoes, halved

½ cup mayonnaise

salt and pepper (optional)

1. Coarsely slice the salad greens. Steam for 3 minutes, then drain and rinse under cold running water, squeezing out as much liquid as possible.

2. Combine the cooked greens with the peas, beans, onion, mint, egg, and salt and pepper, if using. Mix thoroughly with a fork. Stir in the bread crumbs, mixing well. Let stand at room temperature for 30 minutes.

3. Divide the mixture into eight ½-inch-thick patties, each 2½ inches in diameter, firming the edges well.

4. Heat the oil in a nonstick skillet over medium–high heat. Working in batches, add the patties and cook for 2½–3 minutes on each side, turning carefully, until golden and crisp. Meanwhile, preheat the broiler to medium.

5. Toast the pita bread halves under the preheated broiler. Stuff each half with a bean burger, cherry tomato halves, and a dollop of mayonnaise. Serve immediately.

PER SERVING: 294 CAL | FAT: 17 G | SAT FAT: 2.4 G | CARBS: 28.4 G | SUGARS: 3 G | FIBER: 5 G | PROTEIN: 7.6 G | SODIUM: 280 MG

VEGAN SMOKY MUSHROOM & CILANTRO BURGERS

THE SMOKINESS OF THE PAPRIKA COMPLEMENTS THE MUSHROOMS AND RED KIDNEY BEANS PERFECTLY.

PREP TIME: 15 MINUTES | COOK TIME: 10–15 MINUTES | SERVES: 6

1⅔ cups drained and rinsed, canned red kidney beans

2 tablespoons sunflower oil, for frying

1 onion, finely chopped

1⅔ cups finely chopped mushrooms

1 large carrot, shredded

2 teaspoons smoked paprika

1 cup rolled oats

3 tablespoons dark soy sauce

2 tablespoons tomato paste

¾ cup chopped fresh cilantro, including the stems

3 tablespoons all-purpose flour

3 tablespoons sunflower oil, for brushing

6 Boston lettuce leaves

6 vegan burger buns, halved

1 avocado, peeled, pitted, and sliced (optional)

tomato salsa (optional)

salt and pepper (optional)

1. Put the beans into a large bowl and mash as thoroughly as you can with a potato masher. Heat the oil in a skillet, add the onion, and sauté for 2 minutes, until translucent. Add the mushrooms, carrot, and paprika and sauté for an additional 4 minutes, until the vegetables are soft.

2. Add the fried vegetables to the beans with the oats, soy sauce, tomato paste, and cilantro. Season with salt and pepper, if using, and mix well. Divide into six equal portions and shape into patties, then turn in the flour to coat lightly.

3. Preheat a ridged grill pan until smoking. Lightly brush the tops of the patties with oil, then place, oiled side down, on the pan. Cook over medium heat for 2–3 minutes, until lightly charred underneath. Lightly brush the tops with oil, turn, and cook for an additional 2-3 minutes on the other side.

4. Place lettuce on the bottom of each bun, top with a burger, some avocado slices, tomato salsa, if using, and the bun lid. Serve immediately.

PER SERVING: 390 CAL | FAT: 15.9 G | SAT FAT: 1.9 G | CARBS: 49.7 G | SUGARS: 6 G | FIBER: 7.3 G | PROTEIN: 12.1 G | SODIUM: 680 MG

LENTIL BURGERS

THE WHOLE FAMILY—WHETHER VEGETARIAN OR NOT—WILL ENJOY THESE BURGERS MADE FROM TASTY GREEN LENTILS THREADED THROUGH WITH DEEP-GREEN SPINACH.

PREP TIME: 20 MINUTES | COOK TIME: 25 MINUTES | SERVES: 4

1 floury potato, such as russet, cut into ¾-inch cubes

3½ cups baby spinach leaves

1¼ cups cooked Puy lentils or other cooked green lentils

1 onion, coarsely chopped

1½ cups coarsely chopped cremini mushrooms

1 heaping tablespoon chopped fresh parsley

2 teaspoons fresh thyme leaves

1 medium egg, beaten

1½ tablespoons extra virgin canola oil

4 whole-wheat burger buns, halved

3 tablespoons light mayonnaise

2 large tomatoes, sliced

8½ cups mixed salad greens

salt and pepper (optional)

1. Bring a small saucepan of water to a boil. Add the potatoes, bring back to a boil, and cook for 10 minutes, until soft. Drain thoroughly, then return to the stove with the heat turned off. The residual heat will dry out any remaining moisture—shake the pan to help.

2. Meanwhile, put the spinach in a microwavable bowl and microwave on High (850 watts) for 1½ minutes, or until thoroughly wilted. Transfer to a strainer and push all the moisture out using the end of a rolling pin or a pestle. Dry again on paper towels.

3. Put the potatoes, lentils, onion, mushrooms, 1 teaspoon of salt, and pepper, if using, in a food processor and process for 1 minute to a semi-smooth mixture with some texture. Stir the spinach, parsley, and thyme into the mixture by hand, then stir in the egg. Shape into four large ½-inch-thick patties.

4. Heat the oil in a large, nonstick skillet. Add the patties and cook, in batches if necessary, over medium heat for 3 minutes on each side. You may need to reduce the heat to low for the last minute of cooking on each side to prevent the burgers from overbrowning.

5. Spread the burger buns with the mayonnaise. Place the burgers in the buns with the tomato slices and serve immediately with the salad greens on the side.

PER SERVING: 363 CAL | FAT: 12.6 G | SAT FAT: 2.1 G | CARBS: 47.5 G | SUGARS: 4.4 G | FIBER: 11.2 G | PROTEIN: 18 G | SODIUM: 880 MG

VEGAN CHICKPEA WALNUT PATTIES

THESE HEARTY PATTIES ARE SIMILAR TO FALAFEL, BUT THEY HAVE THE ADDED RICHNESS AND FLAVOR OF WALNUTS.

PREP TIME: 20 MINUTES, PLUS CHILLING | COOK TIME: 10 MINUTES | SERVES: 4

2 garlic cloves

1 shallot

1⅔ cups drained and rinsed, canned chickpeas

¼ cup fresh flat-leaf parsley

1 teaspoon ground coriander

1 teaspoon ground cumin

½ teaspoon salt

¾ teaspoon cayenne pepper

2 tablespoons olive oil

2 tablespoons all-purpose flour

½ teaspoon baking powder

½ cup roasted, unsalted walnuts

2 tablespoons sunflower oil, for frying

4 sesame seed burger buns, halved

4 Boston lettuce leaves

2 large tomatoes, sliced

¼ cup vegan mayonnaise (optional)

1. Put the garlic and shallot into a food processor and pulse to chop. Add the chickpeas, parsley, coriander, cumin, salt, cayenne pepper, olive oil, and flour and pulse to a chunky puree. Add the baking powder and pulse once to incorporate. Add the walnuts and pulse once to incorporate.

2. Shape the chickpea mixture into four equal patties, about 4 inches in diameter. Chill in the refrigerator for at least 30 minutes or overnight.

3. Heat the sunflower oil in a large skillet over medium–high heat. Add the patties and cook for 4–5 minutes on each side, until golden brown.

4. Serve hot, layered in the buns with lettuce, tomato slices, and vegan mayonnaise, if using.

PER SERVING: 320 CAL | FAT: 24.7 G | SAT FAT: 2.6 G | CARBS: 18.1 G | SUGARS: 3.5 G | FIBER: 5.2 G | PROTEIN: 7 G | SODIUM: 360 MG

VEGAN MUSHROOM, SPINACH & RICE BURGERS

MADE WITH BROWN RICE, BEANS, AND VEGETABLES, THESE HEALTHY VEGAN BURGERS ARE SATISFYING AND DELICIOUS, SERVED ATOP LARGE PORTOBELLO MUSHROOMS.

PREP TIME: 20 MINUTES, PLUS CHILLING | COOK TIME: 50 MINUTES | SERVES: 4

2¼ tablespoons brown rice

¼ cup olive oil

3 garlic cloves, crushed

4¼ cups chopped button mushrooms

6 cups fresh spinach leaves

1 cup drained and rinsed, canned cranberry beans

1 orange bell pepper, seeded, peeled, and finely chopped

½ cup slivered almonds

2 tablespoons chopped fresh basil

1¼ cups fresh whole-wheat bread crumbs

2 tablespoons whole-wheat flour

2 large tomatoes, sliced

4 large portobello mushrooms

salt and pepper (optional)

1. Cook the rice in a saucepan of boiling water for 20–25 minutes, or according to the package directions, until tender. Drain and place in a food processor.

2. Heat 1 tablespoon of the oil in a skillet. Add the garlic and button mushrooms and cook for 5 minutes. Add to the rice in the food processor.

3. Reserve 1 cup of the spinach leaves. Add the remaining spinach, the beans, orange bell pepper, almonds, basil, bread crumbs, and salt and pepper, if using, to the rice mixture in the food processor and pulse to finely chop. Mix well, then shape into four equal patties. Coat in the flour, then cover and chill in the refrigerator for 1 hour.

4. Preheat the broiler to medium–high. Heat 2 tablespoons of the oil in a nonstick skillet, add the patties, and cook for 5–6 minutes each side, or until golden and cooked through. Meanwhile, brush the tomato slices and portobello mushrooms with the remaining oil and broil for 6–8 minutes, turning once, until soft.

5. Put the reserved spinach leaves on individual serving plates and top each with a mushroom. Add a burger and tomato slice and serve immediately.

PER SERVING: 378 CAL | FAT: 22.3 G | SAT FAT: 2.6 G | CARBS: 32.7 G | SUGARS: 7.3 G | FIBER: 10 G | PROTEIN: 14.5 G | SODIUM: 80 MG

POTATO, BLUE CHEESE & APPLE BURGERS

THE SWEETNESS OF THE APPLE COMPLEMENTS THE STRONG FLAVOR OF THE BLUE CHEESE TO CREATE A UNIQUE AND APPETIZING BURGER.

PREP TIME: 12 MINUTES, PLUS CHILLING | COOK TIME: 25–35 MINUTES | SERVES: 4

6 ounces new potatoes

2 cups mixed nuts, such as pecans, almonds, and hazelnuts

1 onion, coarsely chopped

2 small apples, peeled, cored, and grated

1 cup crumbled vegetarian blue cheese, such as Stilton

1¼ cups fresh whole-wheat bread crumbs

2 tablespoons whole-wheat flour

2 tablespoons sunflower oil, for brushing

baby lettuce leaves (optional)

4 cheese-topped burger buns, halved

½ red onion, thinly sliced

salt and pepper (optional)

1. Cook the potatoes in a saucepan of boiling water for 15–20 minutes, or until tender. Drain and, using a potato masher, crush into small pieces. Put into a large bowl.

2. Put the nuts and onion in a food processor or blender and, using the pulse button, chop finely. Add the nuts, onion, apple, cheese, and bread crumbs to the potatoes in the bowl. Season with salt and pepper, if using. Mix well, then shape into four equal patties. Coat in the flour, then cover and let chill in the refrigerator for 1 hour.

3. Preheat the barbecue grill to medium–high. Brush the patties with the oil and cook for 5–6 minutes on each side, or until cooked through.

4. Put the lettuce leaves on the bottom halves of the buns, if using, and top with the burgers. Add some red onion slices, add the lids, and serve immediately.

PER SERVING: 948 CAL | FAT: 69.1 G | SAT FAT: 17.9 G | CARBS: 61.5 G | SUGARS: 12.3 G | FIBER: 9.9 G | PROTEIN: 27.9 G | SODIUM: 680 MG

VEGAN FALAFEL BURGERS

FALAFEL BURGERS MAKE AN EASY, HEALTHY LUNCH OR DINNER ANY DAY OF THE WEEK, ANY TIME OF YEAR.

PREP TIME: 15 MINUTES | COOK TIME: 4 MINUTES | SERVES: 4

3 cups canned chickpeas, drained and rinsed

1 small onion, chopped

juice and grated zest of 1 unwaxed lime

2 teaspoons ground coriander

2 teaspoons ground cumin

6 tablespoons all-purpose flour

¼ cup olive oil

1 cup fresh watercress sprigs or other peppery greens

prepared vegan tomato salsa, (optional)

1. Put the chickpeas, onion, lime juice and zest, and the spices into a food processor and process to a coarse paste.

2. Turn out onto a clean work surface and shape into four equal patties.

3. Spread out the flour on a large flat plate and turn the patties in it to coat.

4. Heat the oil in a large skillet, add the patties, and cook for 2 minutes on each side, until crisp.

5. Serve immediately with the watercress and tomato salsa, if using.

PER SERVING: 334 CAL | FAT: 16.3 G | SAT FAT: 2 G | CARBS: 34.6 G | SUGARS: 6.9 G | FIBER: 8.8 G | PROTEIN: 9.7 G | TRACE SODIUM

VEGETARIAN CHILI BURGERS

YOU CAN MAKE THESE VEGGIE BURGERS AS SPICY AS YOU WANT BY ADDING MORE OR LESS JALAPEÑO CHILES.

PREP TIME: 25 MINUTES, PLUS CHILLING | COOK TIME: 20 MINUTES | SERVES: 4

⅔ cup bulgur wheat

1 cup drained and rinsed, canned red kidney beans

1 cup drained and rinsed, canned cannellini beans

1 fresh jalapeño chile, seeded and coarsely chopped

2 garlic cloves, coarsely chopped

6 scallions, coarsely chopped

1 yellow bell pepper, peeled, seeded, and chopped

1 tablespoon chopped fresh cilantro

1 cup shredded vegetarian cheddar cheese

2 tablespoons whole-wheat flour

2 tablespoons sunflower oil

1 large tomato, sliced

4 whole-wheat buns, halved

salt and pepper (optional)

1. Put the bulgur wheat into a fine-mesh strainer and rinse under cold running water. Transfer the bulgur wheat to a saucepan of water and cook for 12 minutes, or according to the package directions, until tender. Drain and reserve.

2. Put the beans into a food processor with the chile, garlic, scallions, yellow bell pepper, cilantro, and half the cheese. Using the pulse button, chop finely. Add to the cooked bulgur wheat with salt and pepper, if using. Mix well, then shape into four equal patties. Cover and chill in the refrigerator for 1 hour.

3. Coat the patties in the flour. Preheat the broiler to medium. Heat a heavy skillet and add the oil. When hot, add the patties and cook over medium heat for 5–6 minutes on each side, or until piping hot.

4. Place two slices of tomato on top of each burger and sprinkle with the remaining cheese. Cook under the hot broiler for 2–3 minutes, or until the cheese begins to melt. Serve in the whole-wheat buns.

PER SERVING: 536 CAL | FAT: 19.9 G | SAT FAT: 6.8 G | CARBS: 64.4 G | SUGARS: 7.2 G | FIBER: 14.1 G | PROTEIN: 24.2 G | SODIUM: 440 MG

CHAPTER FOUR

FISH

SALMON QUINOA BURGERS

MADE WITH SALMON, QUINOA, AND EGG, THESE BURGERS ARE FULL OF PROTEIN. TOPPED WITH SPICY MAYONNAISE AND A SPRITZ OF LIME JUICE, YOU'LL BE HARD-PRESSED TO FIND A TASTIER BURGER.

PREP TIME: 15 MINUTES, PLUS CHILLING | COOK TIME: 20–25 MINUTES | SERVES: 4

¾ cup quinoa

9¾ ounces cooked salmon, broken into flakes

1 egg, beaten

4 scallions, trimmed and sliced

1 tablespoon chopped fresh cilantro

4 whole-wheat burger buns, halved

1 tablespoon olive oil, for frying

1 cup fresh watercress sprigs

¼ cucumber, sliced

salt and pepper (optional)

4 lime wedges, to serve

SPICY MAYONNAISE

2 tablespoons capers, chopped

¼ cup mayonnaise

juice of ½ lime

1. Bring a large saucepan of water to a boil. Add the quinoa and boil for 8–10 minutes. Drain well.

2. Put the quinoa into a bowl with the salmon, egg, scallions, and cilantro. Season with salt and pepper, if using, and mix well.

3. With your hands, shape the mixture into four patties. Place them on a plate and chill in the refrigerator for 20 minutes.

4. Meanwhile, make the spicy mayonnaise. Mix the capers, mayonnaise, and lime juice together in a small bowl. Set aside.

5. Preheat the broiler to medium. Toast the burger buns under the broiler.

6. Heat the olive oil in a skillet and cook the patties over medium heat for 4–5 minutes on each side, until golden.

7. Spread the spicy mayonnaise over the bottom burger halves with a few sprigs of watercress and some slices of cucumber. Top with the burgers and sandwich with the second bun halves.

8. Serve with lime wedges for squeezing over the salmon burgers.

PER SERVING: 542 CAL | FAT: 27.3 G | SAT FAT: 4.4 G | CARBS: 48.7 G | SUGARS: 4.1 G | FIBER: 4 G | PROTEIN: 26.1 G | SODIUM: 480 MG

TUNA & WASABI BURGERS

THESE TANTALIZING TUNA BURGERS ARE SERVED ON TOASTED CIABATTA, TOPPED WITH NUTRIENT-RICH, PEPPERY WATERCRESS, WITH JAPANESE-INSPIRED PICKLED VEGETABLES ON THE SIDE.

PREP TIME: 35 MINUTES, PLUS PICKLING | COOK TIME: 20 MINUTES | SERVES: 4

1 pound tuna steaks

½ cup finely chopped fresh cilantro

juice and zest of 1 lime

2 teaspoons wasabi paste

4 scallions, finely chopped

¼ cup mayonnaise

4 whole-wheat ciabatta slices

1 tablespoon olive oil, for brushing

3½ cups watercress

PICKLED VEGETABLES

¼ cup rice wine vinegar

1 tablespoon packed light brown sugar

½ cup water

½ teaspoon coriander seeds, crushed

½ teaspoon mustard seeds

½ cucumber, sliced

2 carrots, cut into matchsticks

6 radishes, thinly sliced

3 shallots, thinly sliced

1. To make the pickled vegetables, first make a pickling liquid. Place the vinegar and sugar with the water into a small saucepan over high heat. Bring to a gentle simmer and stir until the sugar dissolves. Remove from the heat and add the coriander and mustard seeds. Next, place the cucumber, carrots, radish, and shallots into a small bowl or sterilized jar. Pour the pickling liquid over the vegetables, cool and pickle for 4 hours or overnight.

2. Slice the tuna steaks into 1-inch pieces and briefly pulse in a food processor until just chopped. Transfer to a large bowl and combine with the cilantro, lime zest and juice, wasabi paste, scallions, and 2 tablespoons of the mayonnaise. Mix well and put into the refrigerator for 15 minutes.

3. Meanwhile, preheat a ridged grill pan over medium–high heat. Grill the ciabatta slices until toasted and set aside.

4. Shape the tuna mixture into four patty shapes and brush each with oil. Grill for 6 minutes on each side, or until the burgers are cooked through.

5. Serve the tuna burgers on the toasted ciabatta slices, topped with the remaining mayonnaise and the watercress, and with the pickled vegetables on the side.

PER SERVING: 356 CAL | FAT: 10.2 G | SAT FAT: 1.5 G | CARBS: 34.4 G | SUGARS: 10.4 G | FIBER: 4.9 G | PROTEIN: 32.4 G | SODIUM: 440 MG

TRADITIONAL FISH BURGERS

**YOU CAN VARY THE FISH YOU USE TO MAKE THESE BURGERS ACCORDING TO WHAT IS AVAILABLE—
A MIXTURE OF FRESH AND SMOKED FISH PROVIDES A SOPHISTICATED TOUCH.**

PREP TIME: 15 MINUTES, PLUS CHILLING | COOK TIME: 25–30 MINUTES | SERVES: 4

4 Yukon Gold or russet potatoes (about 1 pound), peeled and cut into chunks

1 pound mixed fish fillets, such as cod and salmon, skinned

2 tablespoons chopped fresh tarragon

grated zest of 1 lemon

2 tablespoons heavy cream

1 tablespoon all-purpose flour

1 egg, beaten

2½ cups bread crumbs, made from day-old white or whole-wheat bread

¼ cup vegetable oil, for pan-frying

salt and pepper (optional)

½ cup watercress, to serve

4 lemon wedges, to serve

1. Put the potatoes into a large saucepan of water, bring to a boil, and cook for 15–20 minutes. Drain well and mash with a potato masher until smooth.

2. Meanwhile, put the fish into a skillet and just cover with water. Place over medium heat and bring to a boil, then reduce the heat, cover, and simmer gently for 5 minutes, until cooked.

3. Remove from the heat and drain the fish on a plate. When cool enough to handle, flake the fish into large chunks, making sure there are no bones.

4. Mix the potatoes with the fish, tarragon, lemon zest, and cream. Season well with salt and pepper, if using, and shape into four large patties.

5. Dust the patties with flour and dip them into the beaten egg. Coat thoroughly in the bread crumbs. Place on a baking sheet and chill in the refrigerator for at least 30 minutes.

6. Heat the oil in the skillet and fry the patties over medium heat for 5 minutes on each side, turning them carefully with a spatula.

7. Serve with the watercress, accompanied by the lemon wedges for squeezing over the fish burgers.

PER SERVING: 471 CAL | FAT: 22.3 G | SAT FAT: 5 G | CARBS: 38.9 G | SUGARS: 3 G | FIBER: 3.1 G | PROTEIN: 27.9 G | SODIUM: 240 MG

SALMON BURGERS WITH PINE NUTS

FRESH SALMON, SPINACH, AND PINE NUTS CREATE A COLORFUL AND DELICIOUS BURGER.

PREP TIME: 15 MINUTES, PLUS CHILLING | COOK TIME: 25–35 MINUTES | SERVES: 4

2–3 Yukon Gold or russet potatoes (about 10½ ounces), cut into chunks

1 pound fresh salmon fillet, skinned

6 cups spinach leaves

⅓ cup pine nuts, toasted

2 tablespoons finely grated lemon zest

1 tablespoon chopped fresh parsley

2 tablespoons whole-wheat flour

1 cup crème fraîche or sour cream

1½-inch piece cucumber, peeled and finely chopped

2 tablespoons sunflower oil, for brushing

4 whole-wheat buns, halved

salt and pepper (optional)

28 cherry tomatoes, grilled to serve

1. Cook the potatoes in a saucepan of boiling water for 15–20 minutes, or until tender. Drain well, then mash and reserve. Chop the salmon into chunks.

2. Reserve a few spinach leaves for serving, then blanch the remainder in a saucepan of boiling water for 2 minutes. Drain, squeezing out any excess moisture, then chop.

3. Place the spinach into a food processor or blender with the salmon, potatoes, pine nuts, 1 tablespoon of the lemon zest, the parsley, and salt and pepper, if using. Blend together using the pulse button. Shape into four equal patties, then cover and chill in the refrigerator for 1 hour. Coat the patties in the flour.

4. Mix the crème fraîche, cucumber, and the remaining lemon zest together in a bowl, then cover and chill until required.

5. Preheat the barbecue grill to medium–high. Brush the burgers with the oil and cook for 4–6 minutes on each side, or until cooked through.

6. Place the reserved spinach leaves on the bottom halves of the buns and top with the burgers, then spoon over a little of the crème fraîche mixture. Add the lids and serve immediately with grilled cherry tomatoes.

PER SERVING: 798 CAL | FAT: 49.9 G | SAT FAT: 16.2 G | CARBS: 53 G | SUGARS: 9.1 G | FIBER: 8.5 G | PROTEIN: 37.1 G | SODIUM: 360 MG

CHIPOTLE-LIME SHRIMP BURGERS

THESE BURGERS ARE AN UNEXPECTED WAY TO EAT SHRIMP—AND A LIGHTER OPTION THAN GROUND BEEF.

PREP TIME: 15 MINUTES | COOK TIME: 10 MINUTES | SERVES: 4

1¼ pounds shrimp, peeled and deveined

1 celery stalk, finely diced

2 scallions, finely chopped

2 tablespoons chopped fresh cilantro

1 garlic clove, finely chopped

½ teaspoon salt

½ teaspoon ground chipotle

juice and grated zest of 1 lime

2 teaspoons olive oil

2 tablespoons reduced-fat mayonnaise

4 small whole-wheat burger buns, halved and toasted

4 Boston lettuce leaves

1. Process 1 pound of the shrimp in a food processor. Dice the remaining 4 ounces of shrimp. In a medium bowl, combine the pureed and diced shrimp. Add the celery, scallions, cilantro, garlic, salt, ground chipotle, and lime zest and juice and mix well. Form the mixture into four patties.

2. Heat the oil in a large, nonstick skillet over medium—high heat. Add the shrimp patties and cook for 3—4 minutes or until browned underneath. Flip the patties over and cook for an additional 3—4 minutes or until browned and cooked through.

3. Spread an equal amount of the mayonnaise over the bottom halves of the buns. Place one shrimp patty on the bottom half of each bun, then top with a lettuce leaf and the top half of the bun. Serve immediately.

PER SERVING: 254 CAL | FAT: 7.9 G | SAT FAT: 1.4 G | CARBS: 25.3 G | SUGARS: 3.6 G | FIBER: 3.8 G | PROTEIN: 20 G | SODIUM: 1,120 MG

TUNA BURGERS WITH MANGO SALSA

FRESH TUNA, CHILE, AND MANGO ARE UNITED IN A TOTALLY MODERN BURGER. TUNA IS BEST EATEN SLIGHTLY PINK, SINCE IT CAN BE DRY IF OVERCOOKED.

PREP TIME: 15 MINUTES, PLUS CHILLING | COOK TIME: 25–35 MINUTES | SERVES: 4

1⅔ cups chopped sweet potatoes

1 pound tuna steaks

6 scallions, finely chopped

1½ cups grated zucchini

1 fresh red jalapeño chile, seeded and finely chopped

2 tablespoons mango chutney

1 tablespoon sunflower oil, for brushing

4 Boston lettuce leaves

MANGO SALSA

1 large ripe mango, peeled and pitted

2 ripe tomatoes, finely chopped

1 fresh red jalapeño chile, seeded and finely chopped

1½-inch piece cucumber, finely diced

1 tablespoon chopped fresh cilantro

2 teaspoons honey

1. Cook the sweet potatoes in a saucepan of boiling water for 15–20 minutes, or until tender. Drain well, then mash and put into a food processor or blender. Cut the tuna into chunks and add to the potatoes.

2. Add the scallions, zucchini, chile, and mango chutney to the food processor and, using the pulse button, blend together. Shape into four equal patties, then cover and chill in the refrigerator for 1 hour.

3. Meanwhile make the salsa. Slice the mango, reserving 8–12 slices for serving. Finely chop the remainder, then mix with the tomatoes, chile, cucumber, cilantro, and honey. Mix well, then spoon into a small bowl. Cover and let stand for 30 minutes to let the flavors develop.

4. Preheat the barbecue grill to medium–high. Brush the patties lightly with the oil and cook for 4–6 minutes on each side, or until piping-hot. Serve immediately with the mango salsa, garnished with lettuce leaves and reserved mango slices.

PER SERVING: 316 CAL | FAT: 5.3 G | SAT FAT: 0.8 G | CARBS: 40.5 G | SUGARS: 25.6 G | FIBER: 5.5 G | PROTEIN: 28.4 G | SODIUM: 1,000 MG

POLENTA COD BURGERS WITH HOMEMADE GARLIC MAYONNAISE

PERKED UP WITH BASIL AND FRESH PARMESAN CHEESE, THESE COD BURGERS ARE DEFINITELY TASTY. THE POLENTA—AN ITALIAN-STYLE CORNMEAL—HOLDS ALL THE INGREDIENTS TOGETHER AND IS EASY TO PREPARE.

PREP TIME: 30 MINUTES, PLUS COOLING AND CHILLING | COOK TIME: 18–20 MINUTES | SERVES: 6

1¼ cups water

1⅔ cups instant polenta (or use cornmeal, and follow package directions for preparing)

1 pound cod fillets, skinned

1 tablespoon chopped fresh basil

⅔ cup freshly grated Parmesan cheese

2 tablespoons all-purpose flour

2 tablespoons olive oil, for brushing

6 wedges of ciabatta bread

baby spinach leaves and roasted Mediterranean vegetables (optional)

salt and pepper (optional)

GARLIC MAYONNAISE

3 large garlic cloves, finely chopped

2 egg yolks

1 cup extra virgin olive oil

1 tablespoon lemon juice

1 tablespoon lime juice

1 tablespoon Dijon mustard

1 tablespoon chopped fresh tarragon

salt and pepper (optional)

1. Place the water into a large saucepan and bring to a boil. Slowly pour in the polenta in a steady stream and cook over gentle heat, stirring constantly, for 5 minutes or until thick. Let cool for about 10 minutes.

2. Place the polenta, fish, basil, cheese, and salt and pepper, if using, into a food processor or blender and, using the pulse button, blend together. Shape into six equal patties, then coat in the flour. Cover and chill in the refrigerator for 1 hour.

3. Meanwhile, make the garlic mayonnaise. Make sure all the ingredients are at room temperature. Place the garlic and egg yolks into a food processor and process until well blended. With the motor running, pour in the oil, teaspoon by teaspoon, through the feeder tube until the mixture starts to thicken, then pour in the remaining oil in a thin stream until a thick mayonnaise forms.

4. Add the lemon juice, lime juice, mustard, and tarragon and season with salt and pepper, if using. Blend until smooth, then transfer to a nonmetallic bowl.

5. Cover with plastic wrap and refrigerate until required.

6. Preheat the barbecue grill to medium–high. Brush the patties with the oil and cook for 4–5 minutes on each side, or until cooked through.

7. Place each burger onto a ciabatta wedge and top with a spoonful of garlic mayonnaise. Serve immediately with baby spinach leaves and roasted Mediterranean vegetables.

PER SERVING: 845 CAL | FAT: 51.9 G | SAT FAT: 8.6 G | CARBS: 65 G | SUGARS: 2.4 G | FIBER: 6.2 G | PROTEIN: 27.3 G | SODIUM: 440 MG

TARTAR SAUCE FISH BURGER

THIS BURGER IS MADE WITH MAHI-MAHI, BUT OTHER WHITE FISH, SUCH AS HALIBUT OR TILAPIA, WORK PERFECTLY WHEN MAHI MAHI ISN'T AVAILABLE.

PREP TIME: 20 MINUTES, PLUS CHILLING | COOK TIME: 10 MINUTES | SERVES: 4

4 (6-ounce) mahi-mahi or other white fish fillets

2 teaspoons vegetable or canola oil

4 soft burger buns, halved

½ onion, sliced

4 Boston lettuce leaves

2 large tomatoes, sliced

salt and pepper (optional)

TARTAR SAUCE

2 small pickles, finely chopped

1 scallion, finely chopped

1 tablespoon capers, finely chopped

¼ cup finely chopped fresh flat-leaf parsley

¾ cup mayonnaise

1 tablespoon lemon juice

salt and pepper (optional)

1. To make the tartar sauce, place the pickles, scallion, capers, and parsley into a small bowl and stir in the mayonnaise.

2. Add the lemon juice and stir, then season with salt and pepper, if using. Cover and chill in the refrigerator for at least 30 minutes or up to two days before serving.

3. Rinse the fish and pat dry. Rub the fillets on both sides with the oil and sprinkle with salt and pepper, if using. Place on a large baking sheet.

4. Preheat the broiler to high and place the rack about 3¼ inches below the heat.

5. Place the fish on the rack and cook under the preheated broiler for 4 minutes, then turn and cook for an additional 3 minutes, or until the edges start to brown and the fish is just cooked through (the center of the fish should flake easily when cut into).

6. Spread both halves of each bun with the tartar sauce. Place a fish fillet on each bottom bun half and top with the onion slices, lettuce leaves, and tomato slices. Add the bun lids and serve immediately.

PER SERVING: 635 CAL | FAT: 36.9 G | SAT FAT: 5.8 G | CARBS: 32.5 G | SUGARS: 5.3 G | FIBER: 4.1 G | PROTEIN: 38.5 G | SODIUM: 800 MG

CRAB BURGERS

ONE BITE OF THESE CRAB BURGERS WILL TRANSPORT YOU TO THE BEACH.

PREP TIME: 25 MINUTES, PLUS CHILLING | COOK TIME: 15 MINUTES | SERVES: 6

1 pound crabmeat

⅔ cup mayonnaise

1 tablespoon chopped fresh parsley

1 teaspoon Old Bay seasoning or other seafood seasoning mix

1 egg, beaten

1 teaspoon Worcestershire sauce

1 teaspoon dry mustard

½ teaspoon salt

¼ teaspoon pepper

⅓ cup dried bread crumbs

2 tablespoons butter

6 burger buns, halved

4 Boston lettuce leaves, shredded

2 large tomatoes, sliced

tartar sauce and lemon wedges, to serve (optional)

1. Place the crabmeat into a medium bowl and add the mayonnaise, parsley, Old Bay seasoning, egg, Worcestershire sauce, mustard, salt, and pepper. Gently mix, then add the bread crumbs, a little at a time, and mix gently until combined. Chill in the refrigerator for at least 30 minutes.

2. Divide the mixture into six equal portions and shape each portion into a patty.

3. Heat a ridged grill pan over medium heat, add the butter, and heat until no longer foaming, stirring to coat the bottom of the pan. Add the patties and cook for 6–7 minutes on each side, until golden.

4. Put the patties into the buns and top with the lettuce and tomato slices. Serve immediately with lemon wedges and tartar sauce, if using.

PER SERVING: 452 CAL | FAT: 25.5 G | SAT FAT: 5.9 G | CARBS: 32.4 G | SUGARS: 4.6 G | FIBER: 3.5 G | PROTEIN: 20.8 G | SODIUM: 1,320 MG

SHRIMP & CHIVE BURGERS WITH CORN RELISH

THIS RECIPE COULDN'T BE SIMPLER—OR TASTIER. GENTLY COOKING THE SHRIMP OVER MEDIUM HEAT
HELPS KEEP THEM MOIST AND TENDER ... AND MAKES THEM ABSOLUTELY DELICIOUS.

PREP TIME: 40 MINUTES, PLUS CHILLING | COOK TIME: 30 MINUTES | SERVES: 4

1 pound raw shrimp,
peeled and deveined

½ cup finely chopped chives

1 teaspoon vegetable oil

4 brioche buns, halved

**CORN RELISH
(MAKES ABOUT 4 CUPS)**

3 ears of corn

1 red bell pepper, seeded
and diced

1 jalapeño chile, finely diced

½ apple cider vinegar

½ cup firmly packed
light brown sugar

1 tablespoon salt

1 tablespoon ground mustard seeds

½ teaspoon celery seeds

1 red onion, diced

1. Coarsely chop the shrimp, then put half into a food processor or blender and process until pastelike, or mince with a knife. Stir the paste and chopped shrimp together. Stir the chives into the shrimp.

2. Divide the shrimp mixture into four equal portions. Using damp hands, shape each portion into a patty. Transfer the patties to a plate, cover, and chill in the refrigerator for at least 30 minutes or overnight.

3. Meanwhile, make the corn relish. Cut the kernels off the ears of corn. Put the corn kernels, red bell pepper, chile, vinegar, sugar, salt, mustard seeds, and celery seeds into a large saucepan over medium—high heat and bring to a boil. Reduce the heat to simmering and cook, stirring occasionally, for about 15 minutes, until the mixture reduces slightly. The sugar will melt, producing enough liquid to cover the vegetables.

4. Stir the onion into the corn mixture, remove from the heat, and ladle the relish into sterilized jars. Seal with lids and let cool to room temperature. The relish will keep for up to one month in the refrigerator. Reserve 1 cup the corn relish for the burgers.

5. Heat the oil in a large, nonstick skillet over medium heat and gently place the patties in the pan. Partly cover the pan and cook for 6 minutes, until the patties are almost cooked through. Gently turn and cook on the other side for about 1 minute, until pink and cooked through.

6. Place the burgers in the buns and top each with the reserved corn relish. Serve immediately.

PER SERVING: 391 CAL | FAT: 12.9 G | SAT FAT: 5.9 G | CARBS: 49.1 G | SUGARS: 12.5 G | FIBER: 2.8 G | PROTEIN: 18.3 G | SODIUM: 1,080 MG

CHAPTER FIVE

SAUCES & SIDES

VEGAN KETCHUP

KETCHUP IS AN IMMENSELY POPULAR PANTRY STAPLE, BUT MOST PEOPLE NEVER THINK ABOUT MAKING THEIR OWN. THIS RECIPE IS SURPRISINGLY EASY AND TASTES SUPERB WITH ANY OF THE BURGERS IN THIS BOOK.

PREP TIME: 10 MINUTES | COOK TIME: 15–20 MINUTES | MAKES: ABOUT 1 CUP

2 tablespoons olive oil

1 red onion, chopped

2 garlic cloves, chopped

4 plum tomatoes, chopped

1 cup canned diced tomatoes

½ teaspoon ground ginger

½ teaspoon chili powder

3 tablespoons packed dark brown sugar

½ cup red wine vinegar

salt and pepper (optional)

1. Heat the olive oil in a large saucepan and add the onion, garlic, and all the tomatoes. Add the ginger and chili powder and season with salt and pepper, if using. Cook for 15 minutes, or until soft.

2. Pour the mixture into a food processor or blender and blend well. Strain thoroughly to remove all the seeds. Return the mixture to the pan and add the sugar and vinegar. Return to a boil and cook until it is the consistency of ketchup.

3. Transfer quickly to sterilized jars and store in the refrigerator for up to a month.

PER 1 CUP: 575 CAL | FAT: 28.9 G | SAT FAT: 3.7 G | CARBS: 72.2 G | SUGARS: 58.7 G | FIBER: 6.3 G | PROTEIN: 7 G | SODIUM: 40 MG

VEGAN SPICY SALSA

THIS SPICY, ROASTED SALSA MAKES A GREAT DIP FOR EVERYTHING FROM FRIES TO ONION RINGS, AS WELL AS SPOONING OVER BURGERS.

PREP TIME: 10 MINUTES | COOK TIME: 20 MINUTES | MAKES: ABOUT 2 CUPS

6 sprays of vegetable oil spray

8 plum tomatoes, halved

3 jalapeño peppers, halved, cored, and seeded

4 garlic cloves

1 large onion, cut into wedges

12 sprigs fresh cilantro

¼ cup lime juice

salt (optional)

1. Preheat the oven to 450°F and spray a baking sheet with oil.

2. Put the tomatoes, jalapeño peppers, garlic, and onion onto the prepared baking sheet and lightly spray with oil. Sprinkle with a little salt, if using, and roast in the preheated oven for 15–20 minutes, until the vegetables soften and begin to brown.

3. Put the vegetables into a food processor and pulse to a chunky puree. Add the cilantro, lime juice, and 1 teaspoon of salt, if using, and pulse until the cilantro is chopped and all of the ingredients are well combined.

4. To store, place in sterilized jars and refrigerate for up to 1 week.

PER 2 CUPS: 289 CAL | FAT: 4 G | SAT FAT: 0.1 G | CARBS: 65.1 G | SUGARS: 29.9 G | FIBER: 12.4 G | PROTEIN: 10.5 G | SODIUM: 40 MG

MAYONNAISE

ONE OF THE BASIC SAUCES IN THE FRENCH REPERTOIRE, HOMEMADE MAYONNAISE
HAS A MILDER FLAVOR THAN MOST STORE-BOUGHT TYPES.

PREP TIME: 5 MINUTES | COOK TIME: NO COOKING | MAKES: ABOUT 1¼ CUPS

2 extra-large egg yolks

2 teaspoons Dijon mustard

2 tablespoons lemon juice

1¼ cups sunflower oil

salt and pepper (optional)

1. Process the egg yolks with the Dijon mustard and salt and pepper, if using, in a food processor or blender. Add the lemon juice and process again.

2. With the motor still running, add the oil, drop by drop at first. When the sauce begins to thicken, the oil can then be added in a slow, steady stream. Taste and adjust the seasoning with extra salt, pepper, and lemon juice, if necessary. If the sauce seems too thick, slowly add 1 tablespoon of hot water or lemon juice.

3. Use at once or store in a sterilized, airtight container in the refrigerator for up to 1 week.

PER 1¼ CUPS: 2,774 CAL | FAT: 309.4 G | SAT FAT: 34.1 G | CARBS: 3.8 G | SUGARS: 1 G | FIBER: 0.4 G | PROTEIN: 5.8 G | SODIUM: 160 MG

HOMEMADE MUSTARD

LIKE A SPICY COUNTRY-STYLE DIJON MUSTARD, THIS MUSTARD IS EASY TO MAKE BUT TAKES A FEW DAYS TO FINISH. THE FLAVOR IMPROVES AND BECOMES LESS SPICY AFTER A COUPLE OF DAYS IN THE REFRIGERATOR.

PREP TIME: 15 MINUTES, PLUS DEVELOPING | **COOK TIME:** NO COOKING | **MAKES:** ¾ CUP

3 tablespoons brown mustard seeds

3 tablespoons apple cider vinegar

1–2 tablespoons water

3 tablespoons dry mustard

2 teaspoons salt

2 teaspoons honey

1. Put the mustard seeds into a small, nonmetallic container with the vinegar and enough water to cover completely. Set aside for two days, covered, at room temperature.

2. Strain the mustard seeds, reserving the liquid. Grind in a spice grinder until some seeds are still whole while some are ground. You may have to push the seeds down and grind again, but the more you grind, the spicier the mustard will be.

3. Put the mixture into a small bowl with the dry mustard, salt, and honey. Add the reserved vinegar water and stir.

4. Put into a sterilized jar, seal, and refrigerate for at least 2 days before serving.

PER ¾ CUP: 252 CAL | FAT: 14.8 G | SAT FAT: 0.8 G | CARBS: 18.9 G | SUGARS: 14.2 G | FIBER: 3.8 G | PROTEIN: 10.4 G | SODIUM: 4,800 MG

VEGAN GUACAMOLE

A MEXICAN-STYLE DIP THAT IS DELICIOUS WITH A VARIETY OF THE BURGERS IN THIS BOOK
OR ON THE SIDE FOR DIPPING CHIPS.

PREP TIME: 10 MINUTES | COOK TIME: NO COOKING | SERVES: 4

2 large avocados, pitted, peeled, and sliced

juice of 2 unwaxed limes

2 large garlic cloves, crushed

1 teaspoon mild chili powder, plus extra to garnish

salt and pepper (optional)

1. Put the avocado slices, lime juice, garlic, and chili powder into a food processor and process until smooth. Season with salt and pepper, if using.

2. Transfer to a serving bowl, garnish with chili powder, and serve immediately.

PER SERVING: 170 CAL | FAT: 14.7 G | SAT FAT: 2.1 G | CARBS: 11.1 G | SUGARS: 1.1 G | FIBER: 7.1 G | PROTEIN: 2.3 G | SODIUM: 320 M G

VEGAN BEET HUMMUS

THIS BRIGHTLY COLORED HUMMUS IS PERFECT FOR SPREADING THICKLY ON TOP OF A VEGGIE OR CHICKEN BURGER.

PREP TIME: 15 MINUTES | COOK TIME: NO COOKING | SERVES: 6

1½ cups canned chickpeas, drained and rinsed

1 garlic clove, coarsely chopped

2 cooked beets

1½ tablespoons tahini

juice of ½ unwaxed lemon

3 tablespoons olive oil

salt and pepper (optional)

1. Put the chickpeas, garlic, and beets into a food processor or blender and process until broken into crumbs.

2. Add the tahini and lemon juice and process again, pouring in the oil until the hummus is the consistency you want. Season with salt and pepper, if using, and serve.

PER SERVING: 212 CAL | FAT: 14.3 G | SAT FAT: 1.9 G | CARBS: 15 G | SUGARS: 5.1 G | FIBER: 4.8 G | PROTEIN: 5.3 G | SODIUM 40 MG

VEGAN SPICY SRIRACHA SAUCE

THIS THAI-STYLE SUPERSPICY SAUCE HAS A DELICIOUS FLAVOR WITH JUST THE SAME CHILE HIT
AS STORE-BOUGHT TYPES. PERFECT FOR ADDING AN EXTRASPICY KICK TO YOUR BURGER TOPPINGS.

PREP TIME: 10 MINUTES, PLUS DEVELOPING | COOK TIME: 30 MINUTES | MAKES: ABOUT ¾ CUP

14 red jalapeño, serrano, or
Fresno chiles, stems removed
and halved lengthwise

1 fresh red Thai chile, seeded

8 garlic cloves, coarsely chopped

3 tablespoons packed
light brown sugar

2 tablespoons granulated sugar

2 teaspoons salt

6 tablespoons white wine vinegar

1 teaspoon arrowroot

1. Put all the ingredients, except the vinegar and arrowroot, into a food processor or blender and finely chop. Transfer to a screw-top jar large enough to hold the mixture with space at the top and seal. Let stand at warm room temperature, shaking once a day, for 2–4 days, or until the mixture becomes liquid.

2. Return the mixture to the food processor, add the vinegar, and puree. Strain into a saucepan, rubbing back and forth with a spoon and scraping the strainer to produce as much puree as possible.

3. Turn the stove exhaust fan to high, or open a window to let air circulate. Put the pan over medium heat, bring the puree to a boil, and stir until it is reduced by one-quarter. Reduce the heat to low.

4. Dissolve the arrowroot with 1 tablespoon of the hot liquid, then stir it into the pan. Stir for 30 seconds, until the sauce thickens slightly. Set aside.

5. Let cool, then let mature for 2 weeks in an airtight container in the refrigerator. The sauce will keep for 1 month in the refrigerator.

PER ¾ CUP: 624 CAL | FAT: 3.2 G | TRACE SAT FAT | CARBS: 145.1 G | SUGARS: 108.9 G | FIBER: 1.5 G | PROTEIN: 2.4 G | SODIUM: 4,800 MG

CRISPY ONION RINGS

THE DELICIOUS, CRISPY COATING ON THESE ONION RINGS NICELY COMPLEMENTS THE SWEET TASTE OF THE ONION.

PREP TIME: 5 MINUTES, PLUS STANDING | COOK TIME: 10 MINUTES | SERVES: 2

2 large white onions, peeled

1¼ cups all-purpose flour

1 teaspoon paprika

1 egg

1 cup seltzer water

⅓ cup chopped fresh thyme

½ teaspoon salt

2 tablespoons olive oil

1. Slice the onions into thick rings, then pull apart the sections.

2. In a medium bowl, whisk together the flour, paprika, egg, and seltzer water. Add the thyme and season with salt. Let stand for 5 minutes to thicken.

3. Heat the oil in a large nonstick skillet over medium heat. When the oil is hot, dip the onion rings in the batter, gently shake off the excess batter, then add to the pan. Cook the onion rings on both sides until golden and crispy. You may need to do this in two batches.

4. When the onion rings are cooked, drain on paper towels, then serve immediately.

PER SERVING: 393 CAL | FAT: 15.8 G | SAT FAT: 2.4 G | CARBS: 53.9 G | SUGARS: 6.7 G | FIBER: 4.8 G | PROTEIN: 9.2 G | SODIUM: 440 MG

VEGAN CARAMELIZED ONIONS

SLICED ONIONS, COOKED SLOWLY UNTIL GOLDEN BROWN AND SLIGHTLY SWEET,
ARE A DELICIOUS ACCOMPANIMENT TO ALL KINDS OF BURGERS.

PREP TIME: 5 MINUTES | COOK TIME: 25 MINUTES | SERVES: 4

2 tablespoons vegetable oil

½ red onion, sliced

½ teaspoon chopped fresh
rosemary, thyme, or oregano

½ teaspoon red wine vinegar

salt and pepper (optional)

1. Heat enough oil to coat the bottom of a large skillet over medium heat until shimmering. Add the onion and cook on one side for 3 minutes, until brown. Add the herbs, stir, and continue cooking, stirring occasionally, for about 12 minutes, until nicely browned.

2. Season with salt and pepper, if using. Add the vinegar and cook for an additional 8–10 minutes, until soft.

3. Serve immediately or let cool and store in the refrigerator for up to 3 days.

PER SERVING: 66 CAL | FAT: 6.8 G | SAT FAT: 0.7 G | CARBS: 1.4 G | SUGARS: 0.6 G | FIBER: 0.2 G | PROTEIN: 0.2 G | TRACE SODIUM

VEGAN PICKLED ONIONS

THESE SWEET, SPICY, AND TANGY ONIONS REQUIRE NO HEATING, SO THEY'RE EASY TO MAKE AT ANY TIME. INCLUDE THEM AT THE TABLE WITH ALL YOUR STANDARD BURGER CONDIMENTS.

PREP TIME: 15 MINUTES, PLUS CHILLING | COOK TIME: NONE | MAKES: ABOUT 2 CUPS

1 cup distilled white vinegar

½ cup sugar

1 teaspoon chipotle powder, or to taste

2 red onions, cut into rings

salt (optional)

1. In a medium bowl, combine the vinegar, sugar, chipotle powder, and salt, if using. Whisk to dissolve the sugar.

2. Place the onions in a heavy-duty, zip-top plastic bag and pour the marinade over the onions. Toss to coat. Cover and refrigerate for 30 minutes, moving the mixture around a couple of times to evenly distribute the marinade. Drain before serving.

PER 2 CUPS: 531 CAL | FAT: 0.8 G | SAT FAT: 0.1 G | CARBS: 123.8 G | SUGARS: 110.3 G | FIBER: 4.9 G | PROTEIN: 3.2 G | SODIUM: 40 MG

VEGAN CRANBERRY & RED CABBAGE COLESLAW

THIS VEGAN COLESLAW IS TOSSED WITH A TANGY ORANGE AND OLIVE OIL DRESSING.
IT'S THE PERFECT HEALTHY ALTERNATIVE TO FRIES TO SERVE ALONGSIDE ANY JUICY BURGER.

PREP TIME: 15 MINUTES | COOK TIME: 3 MINUTES | SERVES: 4

1½ cups thinly shredded red cabbage

1 carrot, shredded

1 cup cauliflower florets

1 red-skinned apple, such as Red Delicious, quartered, cored, and thinly sliced

¼ cup dried cranberries

1½ cups alfalfa and radish sprouts

DRESSING

½ cup coarsely chopped walnuts

juice of 1 unwaxed orange

¼ cup virgin olive oil

2 tablespoons chia seeds

salt and pepper (optional)

1. Put the red cabbage, carrot, and cauliflower into a salad bowl. Add the apple, dried cranberries, and sprouts and toss well.

2. To make the dressing, put the walnuts into a large skillet and toast for 2–3 minutes, or until just beginning to brown.

3. Put the orange juice, oil, and chia seeds into a small bowl, season with salt and pepper, if using, then stir in the hot walnuts. Pour the dressing over the salad and toss. Serve immediately or cover and chill in the refrigerator until needed.

PER SERVING: 320 CAL | FAT: 23.2 G | SAT FAT: 2.8 G | CARBS: 29.5 G | SUGARS: 16 G | FIBER: 9.3 G | PROTEIN: 4.9 G | SODIUM: 320 MG

VEGAN SPELT & CARROT SALAD

SERVE THIS HEALTHY SALAD IN A LARGE BOWL AT ANY BARBECUE FOR GUESTS TO ADD AS AN EXTRA TOPPING TO THEIR BURGER, OR FOR ADDED CRUNCH ON THE SIDE.

PREP TIME: 15 MINUTES, PLUS STANDING | COOK TIME: 15 MINUTES | SERVES: 4

1¼ cups pearled spelt, rinsed

½ teaspoon salt

2 tablespoons fresh thyme leaves

⅓ cup toasted pine nuts

5 scallions, thinly sliced

4 carrots

3 tablespoons cress or microgreens, to serve

DRESSING

2 tablespoons orange juice

1 tablespoon lemon juice

¾-inch piece fresh ginger, squeezed in a garlic press, juice reserved

2 teaspoons soy sauce

6 tablespoons extra virgin olive oil

salt and pepper (optional)

1. Put the spelt and salt into a saucepan with plenty of water to cover. Bring to a boil, then reduce the heat, cover, and simmer for 10 minutes, until tender but still chewy. Drain, then spread out on a baking sheet to cool slightly. Transfer to a serving bowl while still lukewarm.

2. To make the dressing, combine the orange juice, lemon juice, and ginger juice in a small bowl. Add the soy sauce. Season with salt and pepper, if using. Whisk in the oil.

3. Pour the dressing over the spelt, mixing gently with a fork. Stir in the thyme, pine nuts, and scallions.

4. Using a vegetable peeler, shave the carrots into thin ribbons, discarding the woody core. Add to the spelt mixture.

5. Let stand at room temperature for 30 minutes to let the flavors develop. Sprinkle with the cress or microgreens just before serving.

PER SERVING: 464 CAL | FAT: 28.2 G | SAT FAT: 3.5 G | CARBS: 48.7 G | SUGARS: 5.4 G | FIBER: 6.2 G | PROTEIN: 9.5 G | SODIUM: 480 MG

ZESTY AVOCADO & ALMOND SALAD

SMOOTH AND TASTY AVOCADOS ARE FLAVORED WITH ZESTY LEMON JUICE, FRAGRANT CILANTRO, PIQUANT SCALLIONS, AND HOT CHILE, AND A SPRINKLING OF SLIVERED ALMONDS ADD AN EXTRA CRUNCH.

PREP TIME: 10–15 MINUTES | COOK TIME: 5 MINUTES | SERVES: 4

2 teaspoons olive oil

½ cup slivered almonds

1 iceberg lettuce, quartered, and torn into bite-size pieces

3 avocados, halved, pitted, and peeled

juice of 2 lemons

DRESSING

¼ cup low-fat plain yogurt

2 scallions, finely chopped

¼ teaspoon crushed red pepper flakes

⅔ cup finely chopped fresh cilantro

salt and pepper (optional)

1. Heat the oil in a skillet over medium heat. Add the almonds and cook for 3–4 minutes, or until golden, stirring often, then let cool.

2. Put the lettuce into a salad bowl. Slice two of the avocados, put them in a bowl, and squeeze the juice of 1½ lemons over them to prevent discoloration. Transfer to the salad bowl.

3. To make the dressing, mash the remaining avocado on a plate with the remaining lemon juice. Mix in the yogurt, scallions, red pepper flakes, and cilantro and season lightly with salt and pepper, if using.

4. Sprinkle the salad with the cooked almonds, then spoon the dressing over the salad. Serve immediately alongside your burgers.

PER SERVING: 289 CAL | FAT: 24 G | SAT FAT: 3.2 G | CARBS: 17.8 G | SUGARS: 5.4 G | FIBER: 9.7 G | PROTEIN: 6.9 G | SODIUM: 40 MG

POTATO SALAD

COOL AND CREAMY, THIS SALAD SHOULD BE AN INTEGRAL PART OF ANY BARBECUE.

PREP TIME: 20 MINUTES, PLUS CHILLING | COOK TIME: 30 MINUTES | SERVES: 8

10–12 white round potatoes (about 2¾ pounds)

½ cup mayonnaise

¼ cup sour cream

⅓ cup white wine vinegar

1 teaspoon whole-grain mustard

½ teaspoon dried dill

½ cup finely chopped red onions

¼ cup finely chopped celery

3 tablespoons chopped pickles

¼ cup chopped roasted red peppers

2 medium hard-boiled eggs, chopped (optional)

salt and pepper (optional)

1. Place the unpeeled potatoes in a medium saucepan and cover with water by a few inches. Add salt, if using, bring to a boil over high heat, then reduce the heat and simmer for 20–30 minutes, until tender.

2. Put the mayonnaise, sour cream, vinegar, mustard, dill, and salt and pepper, if using, into a bowl and mix together.

3. Drain the potatoes and let cool slightly, then slip off the skins with your fingers or with a paring knife. Chop the potatoes into ½-inch pieces and add to the dressing while still warm. Stir in the onion, celery, pickles, roasted peppers, and eggs, if using. Cover and chill for at least 2 hours or overnight.

PER SERVING: 246 CAL | FAT: 13.1 G | SAT FAT: 2.5 G | CARBS: 29.2 G | SUGARS: 2.3 G | FIBER: 3.6 G | PROTEIN: 3.7 G | SODIUM: 160 MG

MACARONI & CHEESE

THIS SATISFYING FAVORITE GOES WELL WITH ANY BURGER. SPOON ON TOP OF YOUR PATTY OF CHOICE FOR ADDED FLAVOR AND CREAMY TEXTURE.

PREP TIME: 10 MINUTES | COOK TIME: 35 MINUTES | SERVES: 4

9 ounces dried elbow macaroni

4½ tablespoons butter

2½ cups milk

½ teaspoon grated nutmeg

½ cup all-purpose flour

1¾ cups shredded cheddar cheese

⅔ cup freshly grated Parmesan cheese

salt and pepper (optional)

1. Bring a large saucepan of water to a boil. Add the pasta, bring back to a boil, and cook for 8–10 minutes, or until tender but still firm to the bite. Remove from the heat and drain. Add ½ tablespoon of the butter, return to the pan, and cover to keep warm.

2. Put the milk and nutmeg into a separate saucepan over low heat and heat until warm, but do not bring to a boil.

3. Melt the remaining 4 tablespoons of butter in a heavy saucepan over low heat, then add the flour and stir to make a roux. Cook gently for 2 minutes.

4. Add the milk a little at a time, whisking it into the roux, then cook for an additional 10–15 minutes to make a loose, gravy-like sauce.

5. Add three-quarters of the cheddar cheese and all the Parmesan cheese and stir through until they have melted in. Season with salt and pepper, if using, then remove from the heat.

6. Preheat the broiler to high. Put the macaroni into a shallow heatproof dish, then pour the sauce over the pasta.

7. Sprinkle the remaining cheese over the top and place the dish under the preheated broiler. Broil until the cheese begins to brown. Serve immediately.

PER SERVING: 743 CAL | FAT: 38.8 G | SAT FAT: 23.5 G | CARBS: 66.5 G | SUGARS: 9.6 G | FIBER: 2.4 G | PROTEIN: 30.8 G | SODIUM: 680 MG

BURGER BUNS

THE BUNS ARE JUST AS IMPORTANT AS THE BURGERS INSIDE THEM. YOU'LL DEFINITELY NOTICE THE DIFFERENCE FROM STORE-BOUGHT BUNS WHEN YOU BITE INTO THESE DELIGHTS.

PREP TIME: 20 MINUTES, PLUS RESTING | COOK TIME: 15–20 MINUTES | MAKES: 8 BUNS

3⅓ cups white bread flour

1½ teaspoons salt

2 teaspoons sugar

1 teaspoon active dry yeast

⅔ cup lukewarm water

⅔ cup lukewarm milk

4 teaspoons white bread flour, for dusting

1 tablespoon vegetable oil, for brushing

3 tablespoons sesame seeds

1. Sift the flour and salt together into a bowl and stir in the sugar and yeast. Make a well in the center and pour in the lukewarm water and milk. Stir well with a wooden spoon until the dough begins to come together, then knead with your hands until it leaves the side of the bowl. Turn out onto a lightly floured surface and knead well for about 10 minutes, until smooth and elastic.

2. Brush a bowl with oil. Shape the dough into a ball, put it into the bowl, and put the bowl into a plastic bag or cover with a damp dish towel. Let rise in a warm place for 1 hour, until the dough has doubled in volume.

3. Brush two baking sheets with oil. Turn out the dough onto a lightly floured surface and punch down with your heel of your hand. Divide it into eight equal pieces, shape each into a ball, and put them onto the prepared baking sheets. Flatten slightly with a lightly floured hand and put the baking sheets into plastic bags or cover with damp dish towels. Let rise in a warm place for 30 minutes.

4. Preheat the oven to 400°F. Lightly press the center of each bun with your fingers to release any large air bubbles. Brush the tops with the oil and sprinkle with sesame seeds. Bake for 15–20 minutes, until light golden brown. Transfer to wire racks to cool.

PER SERVING: 260 CAL | FAT: 4.8 G | SAT FAT: 0.9 G | CARBS: 43.1 G | SUGARS: 2.5 G | FIBER: 1.9 G | PROTEIN: 10.2 G | SODIUM: 440 MG

BUTTERMILK BURGER BUNS

THESE SLIGHTLY SWEET AND SOFT-TEXTURED BUNS WILL SANDWICH ANY BURGER PERFECTLY.

PREP TIME: 30 MINUTES, PLUS RESTING | COOK TIME: 10–20 MINUTES | MAKES: 8 PIECES

3 cups white bread flour

1¼ cups all-purpose flour

7 tablespoons butter, diced

1 extra-large egg

2 tablespoons sugar

2¼ teaspoons active dry yeast

1¼ cups buttermilk

1 teaspoon salt

4 teaspoons all-purpose flour, for dusting

1 egg, lightly beaten, for glazing

1. In a large bowl, mix the white bread flour and all-purpose flour together and rub in the butter until the mixture resembles fine bread crumbs.

2. In a medium bowl, whisk together the egg, sugar, yeast, buttermilk, and salt.

3. Pour the egg mixture into the flour mixture and combine using the back of a wooden spoon. Turn out the dough onto a floured surface and knead for 10 minutes, or until elastic and smooth.

4. Place the dough in a clean bowl, cover with plastic wrap, and let rise in a warm place for 1½ hours.

5. Punch down the dough with the heel of your hand, then turn out onto a floured surface. Divide the mixture into eight pieces. Roll each piece into a ball and put onto a large baking sheet, spaced well apart to let the buns double in size.

6. Cover the baking sheet with plastic wrap and let rise in a warm place for 30–40 minutes, or until doubled in size. Preheat the oven to 350°F.

7. Lightly brush the buns with the beaten egg and bake in the preheated oven for 15–20 minutes.

PER SERVING: 403 CAL | FAT: 13.7 G | SAT FAT: 7.7 G | CARBS: 56 G | SUGARS: 5.9 G | FIBER: 2 G | PROTEIN: 13.1 G | SODIUM: 440 MG

VEGAN HAND-CUT FRIES

CRISPY HAND-CUT FRIES ARE THE PERFECT ACCOMPANIMENT TO ANY BURGER. COOKING THEM IN THE OVEN IS MUCH HEALTHIER THAN FRYING.

PREP TIME: 10 MINUTES | COOK TIME: 30 MINUTES | SERVES: 4

8 russet potatoes (about 2 pounds), cut into even sticks

2 tablespoons vegetable oil

1 teaspoon sea salt

1. Preheat the oven to 450°F.

2. Toss the cut potatoes with vegetable oil and sea salt.

3. Spread the potatoes in a single layer on a large baking sheet and bake in the preheated oven for about 30 minutes, flipping them halfway through cooking, until they are golden brown and crisp.

4. Serve immediately alongside your burger of choice.

PER SERVING: 233 CAL | FAT: 7 G | SAT FAT: 0.7 G | CARBS: 39.3 G | SUGARS: 1.8 G | FIBER: 4.7 G | PROTEIN: 4.6 G | SODIUM: 600 MG

VEGAN GARLIC FRIES

TRADITIONAL HAND-CUT FRIES HIT WITH A DOSE OF FRESH GARLIC AND A SPRINKLING OF CHOPPED PARSLEY.

PREP TIME: 15 MINUTES | COOK TIME: 30 MINUTES | SERVES: 4

8 russet potatoes (about 2 pounds)

2 tablespoons vegetable oil

1 teaspoon sea salt

1 tablespoon olive oil

3 large garlic cloves, finely chopped

2 tablespoons finely chopped fresh flat-leaf parsley

sea salt (optional)

1. Preheat the oven to 450°F. Peel the potatoes, if desired, and cut into even sticks.

2. Toss the potatoes with vegetable oil and sea salt.

3. Spread the potatoes in a single layer on a large baking sheet and bake in the preheated oven for about 30 minutes, flipping them halfway through cooking, until they are golden brown and crisp.

4. Whisk together the oil, garlic, and parsley in a large bowl.

5. Toss the hot fries with the garlic mixture. Season generously with sea salt, if using, and serve immediately alongside your burger of choice.

PER SERVING: 267 CAL | FAT: 10.4 G | SAT FAT: 1.2 G | CARBS: 40.2 G | SUGARS: 1.9 G | FIBER: 4.8 G | PROTEIN: 4.8 G | SODIUM: 600 MG

SMOKY PAPRIKA SWEET POTATO FRIES

STARCHY AND SWEET, WITH CRUNCHY EDGES AND FLUFFY INSIDES, THESE FRIES MAKE A REALLY SATISFYING ACCOMPANIMENT TO ANY BURGER. ALWAYS USE THE BEST PAPRIKA YOU CAN FIND.

PREP TIME: 10 MINUTES | COOK TIME: 40 MINUTES | SERVES: 2

2 sweet potatoes, unpeeled, scrubbed, and cut into sticks

2 tablespoons olive oil

1 heaping tablespoon smoked paprika

sea salt and pepper (optional)

SOUR CREAM DIP

4 stems of chives, finely snipped

⅔ cup sour cream

salt and pepper (optional)

1. Preheat the oven to 350°F. Put the sweet potatoes, oil, and smoked paprika into a large bowl, season with salt and pepper, if using, and toss well.

2. Arrange the fries in a single layer on a large baking sheet. Bake for 30–40 minutes, or until crisp.

3. To make the dip, put the chives and sour cream into a bowl and mix. Season with salt and pepper, if using, and divide between two small dipping bowls.

4. Line two larger bowls with paper towels. Transfer the fries to the bowls and serve immediately with the dip alongside your burger of choice.

PER SERVING: 399 CAL | FAT: 28.4 G | SAT FAT: 10.4 G | CARBS: 32.8 G | SUGARS: 8.8 G | FIBER: 5 G | PROTEIN: 4 G | SODIUM: 440 MG

THAI RED FRIES

THESE UNUSUAL OVEN-BAKED FRIES HIT ALL THE RIGHT TASTE BUDS—SWEET, SPICY, TANGY, SALTY, AND ALL-AROUND DELICIOUS.

PREP TIME: 15 MINUTES | COOK TIME: 30 MINUTES | SERVES: 4

2 tablespoons vegetable oil, plus 1 tablespoon for greasing

2 tablespoons packed light brown sugar

2 tablespoons Thai fish sauce

2 tablespoons lime juice

1 tablespoon Thai red curry paste

½ teaspoon cayenne pepper (optional)

8 russet potatoes (about 2 pounds), cut into even sticks

CILANTRO KETCHUP

1 garlic clove

6 sprigs fresh cilantro

1 cup ketchup

2 tablespoons lime juice

1. Preheat the oven to 450°F. Grease a large baking sheet with oil.

2. Put the oil, sugar, fish sauce, lime juice, curry paste, and cayenne pepper, if using, into a mixing bowl and stir together until well combined.

3. Add the potato sticks to the mixture in the bowl and toss to coat. Let stand for about 5 minutes, then, using a slotted spoon, transfer the potatoes to the prepared baking sheet, letting the excess marinade run off into the bowl. Spread the potatoes in a single layer. Bake in the preheated oven for 25–30 minutes, turning after about 15 minutes, until brown and crisp.

4. Meanwhile, to make the ketchup, chop the garlic and cilantro in a food processor. Add the ketchup and lime juice and process until well combined. Transfer to a serving bowl.

5. Serve the fries hot, with the ketchup for dipping, alongside your burger of choice.

PER SERVING: 366 CAL | FAT: 10.9 G | SAT FAT: 1.1 G | CARBS: 65.5 G | SUGARS: 22.3 G | FIBER: 5.4 G | PROTEIN: 5.9 G | SODIUM: 1,360 MG

VEGAN STUFFED POTATO SKINS

SERVE THESE VEGAN POTATO SKINS ALONGSIDE YOUR BURGERS FOR A FILLING DINNER OPTION.

PREP TIME: 10–15 MINUTES | COOK TIME: 35 MINUTES | SERVES: 2

1 tablespoon vegetable oil, for greasing

2 russet potatoes

2 tablespoons olive oil, for brushing and frying

3 vegan bacon-style strips

1 tablespoon chopped fresh mixed herbs, such as sage, parsley, oregano

½ tablespoon vegan margarine

salt and pepper (optional)

1. Preheat the oven to 375°F. Lightly grease a baking sheet with the vegetable oil.

2. Score a ring around each potato, in the place where you will eventually cut them in half. Wrap them in paper towels and microwave for 6–10 minutes, or until cooked through. Unwrap and let stand until cool enough to handle. Cut the potatoes in half and carefully scoop out the flesh, leaving a shell around ½ inch thick. Set the flesh aside in a medium bowl.

3. Brush the outside of the potato skins with 1 tablespoon olive oil and place them, cut side down, on the prepared baking sheet. Bake in the preheated oven for 15 minutes, or until browned, then remove from the oven and transfer to a clean baking sheet, cut side up.

4. Heat the remaining olive oil in a skillet over medium heat. Cook the vegan bacon strips for 5 minutes, or until crisp, and then chop finely or crumble them. Mash the reserved potato flesh with a fork, and then mix in the vegan bacon and chopped herbs. Season with salt and pepper, if using.

5. Preheat the broiler to high. Pile the mashed potato back into the potato skins, make ridges on top with a fork, and dot with a little vegan margarine. Place under the hot broiler for 5 minutes, until the tops are golden and crisp. Serve immediately.

PER SERVING: 460 CAL | FAT: 25.5 G | SAT FAT: 4.4 G | CARBS: 46 G | SUGARS: 2.1 G | FIBER: 6.8 G | PROTEIN: 13.1 G | SODIUM: 200 MG

BACON & CHEESE LOADED FRIES

THESE LOADED FRIES ARE PUMPED FULL OF FLAVOR WITH ONION, GARLIC, TWO KINDS OF CHEESE, CRUMBLED BACON, AND FRESH CHIVES.

PREP TIME: 15 MINUTES | COOK TIME: 45 MINUTES | SERVES: 4

3 bacon strips

3 tablespoons butter

½ onion, diced

1 garlic clove, finely chopped

3 tablespoons all-purpose flour

1½ cups milk

2⅓ cups shredded sharp cheddar cheese

⅔ cup freshly grated Parmesan cheese

½ cup sour cream

2 teaspoons Dijon mustard

salt (optional)

2 tablespoons snipped fresh chives, to garnish

HAND-CUT FRIES

8 russet potatoes, about 2 pounds, cut into even sticks

2 tablespoons vegetable oil

1 teaspoon sea salt

1. Preheat the oven to 450°F. Fry the bacon in a dry skillet until crisp, then remove and drain on paper towels. Crumble and set aside.

2. Melt the butter in a saucepan over medium heat. Add the onion and cook, stirring, for about 4 minutes, until soft. Add the garlic and cook for an additional minute. Whisk in the flour and cook for an additional 30 seconds. Slowly add the milk and cook over medium heat, whisking constantly, for an additional 3 minutes, until the sauce thickens. Reduce the heat to low and add the cheddar cheese and Parmesan cheese about ¼ cup at a time, stirring after each addition, until the cheese is completely melted. Stir in the sour cream, mustard, and salt, if using. Keep the sauce warm until ready to serve.

3. To make the hand-cut fries, toss the potatoes with vegetable oil and sea salt.

4. Spread the potatoes in a single layer on a large baking sheet and bake in the preheated oven for about 30 minutes, flipping them halfway through cooking, until they are golden brown and crisp.

5. Place the fries in a large bowl or on a serving platter and pour the sauce over them. Sprinkle with the crumbled bacon and chives and serve immediately.

PER SERVING: 820 CAL | FAT: 53.7 G | SAT FAT: 27.4 G | CARBS: 53.8 G | SUGARS: 8.3 G | FIBER: 5.2 G | PROTEIN: 32.2 G | SODIUM: 1,520 MG

VEGAN BUTTERNUT SQUASH WITH SAGE & PUMPKIN SEEDS

A HEALTHY AND COLORFUL ALTERNATIVE TO A SIDE PORTION OF FRIES.

PREP TIME: 20 MINUTES | COOK TIME: 35 MINUTES | SERVES: 3

1 large butternut squash

1 tablespoon olive oil

½ teaspoon chili powder

12 fresh sage leaves, finely chopped

⅓ cup pumpkin seeds

salt and pepper (optional)

1. Preheat the oven to 400°F. Prepare the butternut squash by washing any excess dirt from the skin and slicing off the top and bottom ends.

2. Using a sharp knife and a steady hand, cut the squash into six long wedges. Scoop out any seeds and discard. Place the wedges on a baking pan. Brush with half of the olive oil and sprinkle with the chili powder. Roast in the preheated oven for 25 minutes.

3. Remove from the oven and brush with the remaining olive oil. Sprinkle the sage and pumpkin seeds over the squash. Season with salt and pepper, if using, and return the wedges to the oven for an additional 10 minutes. Serve immediately, garnished with extra pepper, if using.

PER SERVING: 259 CAL | FAT: 13.3 G | SAT FAT: 2.1 G | CARBS: 33.9 G | SUGARS: 6.1 G | FIBER: 7.2 G | PROTEIN: 7.8 G | TRACE SODIUM

CHICKPEA TOFU STICKS WITH SPICY DIP

COTTAGE CHEESE IS A FRESH CURD THAT'S DRAINED BUT NOT PRESSED, SO SOME OF THE WHEY REMAINS. AS THE BASE OF A SPICY DIP, IT TASTES AMAZING DUNKED WITH STRIPS OF HOMEMADE TOFU.

PREP TIME: 15 MINUTES, PLUS STANDING AND CHILLING | COOK TIME: 5–6 MINUTES | SERVES: 4

1 cup chickpea (besan) flour
1 teaspoon miso paste
½ teaspoon ground turmeric
2 cups water

SPICY DIP

1⅓ cups cottage cheese
1 tablespoon mayonnaise
2 teaspoons creamed horseradish
½ teaspoon Dijon mustard
1 scallion, trimmed and finely chopped
12 olives, pitted and finely chopped

1. To make the chickpea tofu, put the chickpea flour into a bowl with the miso paste and turmeric. Whisk in 1 cup of the water.

2. Bring the remaining water to a boil in a saucepan. When the water is boiling, pour the chickpea flour mixture into the pan and start whisking.

3. Simmer while stirring constantly, until the mixture thickens. Pour it into a 6-inch-square pan or dish. Let stand at room temperature for 20 minutes, then chill in the refrigerator for at least 30 minutes.

4. Meanwhile, make the dip by combining the ingredients in a small bowl.

5. Cut the tofu into strips and serve with the spicy dip.

PER SERVING: 208 CAL | FAT: 8.9 G | SAT FAT: 1.9 G | CARBS: 18.7 G | SUGARS: 5.9 G | FIBER: 3.2 G | PROTEIN: 13.3 G | SODIUM: 440 MG

VEGAN ROASTED KALE CHIPS

KALE'S MEATY FLAVOR BECOMES WONDERFULLY INTENSE WHEN THE LEAVES ARE ROASTED.
TORN INTO BITE-SIZE PIECES, THEY MAKE CRISPY MORSELS THAT ARE PERFECT SERVED WITH JUICY BURGERS.

PREP TIME: 15 MINUTES | COOK TIME: 15 MINUTES | SERVES: 4

9 ounces kale

2 tablespoons olive oil

2 pinches of sugar

2 pinches of sea salt

2 tablespoons toasted
slivered almonds, to garnish

1. Preheat the oven to 300°F. Remove the thick stems and central rib from the kale (leaving about 2 cups trimmed leaves). Rinse and dry thoroughly with paper towels. Tear into bite-size pieces and place in a bowl with the oil and sugar, then toss well.

2. Spread about half the leaves in a single layer in a large roasting pan, spaced well apart. Sprinkle with a pinch of sea salt and roast on the bottom rack of the preheated oven for 4 minutes.

3. Stir the leaves, then turn the pan so the back is at the front. Roast for an additional 1–2 minutes, until the leaves are crisp and slightly browned at the edges. Repeat with the remaining leaves and sea salt. Sprinkle the kale chips with the slivered almonds and serve immediately.

PER SERVING: 119 CAL | FAT: 9.7 G | SAT FAT: 1.1 G | CARBS: 6.8 G | SUGARS: 2.1 G | FIBER: 2.7 G | PROTEIN: 3.6 G | SODIUM: 320 MG

INDEX